MW01194767

GAME OF MY LIFE

ST. LOUIS

CARDINALS

MEMORABLE STORIES OF CARDINALS BASEBALL

MATTHEW LEACH

WITH STUART SHEA

SPORTS
PUBLISHING

Sports Publishing books may be purchased in bulk at special discounts for sales promotion, corporate gifts, fund-raising, or educational purposes. Special editions can also be created to specifications. For details, contact the Special Sales Department, Sports Publishing, 307 West 36th Street, 11th Floor, New York, NY 10018 or info@skyhorsepublishing.com.

Sports Publishing® is a registered trademark of Skyhorse Publishing, Inc.®, a Delaware corporation.

www.sportspubbooks.com

10 9 8 7 6 5 4 3 2 1

Library of Congress Cataloging-in-Publication Data is available on file.

ISBN: 978-1-61321-072-7

Printed in the United States of America

*For my wife, Erin, whose love, support, and understanding
make me better at everything I do*

CONTENTS

ACKNOWLEDGMENTS

It starts at the beginning. Thank you to my parents, who always supported me but never pushed me, who encouraged my love of words and my love of baseball, and without whom I wouldn't even be a baseball writer in the first place.

Thank you to Mike Pearson, who was persistent in his efforts to sign me up for this project, and to Doug Hoepker, who had just the right touch as an editor.

Martin Coco showed great enthusiasm for the project and opened up his rolodex to help me find the majority of the players contained in this book. Dave Wilhelm and Warren Mayes helped me get in touch with players I might not otherwise have found. Will Carroll provided me with valuable insight about the process and business of writing a book. Brian Bartow was understanding and helpful with access.

Thank you to Jim Banks, Geoff Grant, Dinn Mann, and everyone else at MLB Advanced Media for your support as I added a second job to my full-time job. Thanks to Christine Destefano, who brought me to baseball eight years ago before MLBAM even existed; accepting her offer was easily the best decision of my professional life.

Baseball-reference.com and Retrosheet.org are simply amazing resources, utterly indispensable to any baseball fan, but especially a baseball fan writing a book.

Of course, an enormous thanks to the players themselves, who were generous with their time and insight. Doing the interviews was the best part of this whole project. As a baseball fan, it was a delight to have 20 ballplayers share such special stories.

Molly the dog and Beatrice the cat were my constant companions as I wrote. And my amazing, wonderful, supportive, beautiful, kind, and brilliant wife, Erin, helped in every way she possibly could, and with a greater depth than I could ever have asked. It wouldn't have happened without her; I wouldn't have even tried.

CHAPTER 1

ADAM WAINWRIGHT

When players make their way south to Spring Training in Florida and Arizona in early February, it's tough to envision October. As the boys of summer shed the rust from the winter and resume the routines that stick with them throughout the season, playoff baseball sits pretty far back in their brains. The palm trees, small ballparks, and bright sunshine of the Grapefruit League don't typically conjure thoughts of chilly fall nights in front of 50,000 people and millions more on television.

That's even truer for the rookies and for the prospects trying to crack big-league rosters. For them, day-to-day survival is the goal and Opening Day is the dream. Every day you're not called into the manager's office is a good day. Just be there when the first pitch is thrown out, and you've accomplished something. May, June, and July are bonuses; October borders on the unfathomable.

That was Adam Wainwright's situation when he reported to Jupiter, Florida, in February of 2006. Wainwright, a top prospect in the Cardinals organization, had pitched a grand total of two big-league innings the previous September. That was the extent of his major league experience, and nobody had him even penciled in to add to that experience at the start of the season. Down the road, maybe. But Wainwright looked more like insurance to be stashed at Triple-A Memphis, rather than any kind of factor in St. Louis. In any honest and fair assessment, he was likely seventh among starting pitchers on the Cardinals' depth chart.

Wainwright could scarcely imagine pitching in the playoffs, never mind securing the final out of the National League Championship Series. But that's just where the 8½-month journey of the '06 season took Wainwright. He went from barely in the picture to utterly indispensable, and became an October legend in the process.

At age 24, Wainwright reported to Cardinals camp as a long-shot candidate for the starting rotation. Technically he was part of a competition for the fifth starter's job, but in reality that spot was Sidney Ponson's to lose. Wainwright outpitched Ponson as well as the third candidate, Anthony Reyes, but Ponson didn't lose it, so Wainwright never really had a chance to win it. Still, he was so impressive in the spring that the Cardinals didn't want to send him back to the minors for another tour at Memphis. So Wainwright was kept around as a long reliever. It was the Earl Weaver method of pitcher development—break in a future starter by giving him innings in the bullpen. And given Weaver's success, that's not a bad model to follow.

Wainwright made his 2006 debut pitching the eighth inning of a blowout win on Opening Day in Philadelphia. He often pitched long relief for the first month, going three innings twice and 2⅔ another time. He was getting the unpleasant jobs that fall to the low man on the bullpen totem pole. By June, though, things were starting to change a little bit. His assignments were later, shorter, and in tighter games. The youngster was earning the trust of manager Tony La Russa and pitching coach Dave Duncan. In the second half of the season, Wainwright emerged as a trusted setup man and arguably the team's best reliever.

In early September, closer Jason Isringhausen finally gave up his valiant effort to pitch through a hip injury. He shut it down for surgery with three weeks remaining in the season, leaving the Cardinals without a closer. La Russa would not publicly commit to Wainwright or veteran Braden Looper, and oddly, few save chances presented themselves.

Adam Wainwright progressed from a kid just trying to make the team to World Series closer in the span of seven months. *AP/WWP*

Finally, two critical opportunities arose—and they were both given to Wainwright. He nailed down two of the Cardinals' last three wins of the regular season, and they were both vital as the National League Central race went down to the final day. It was clear that the rookie was the man. That only became clearer and clearer in October.

"Each situation was a growing process for me," Wainwright said. "I got put into bigger situation after bigger situation after bigger situation. So when I was finally put in the biggest situation of all, it really wasn't that much of a difference. At the end, in the last two games I closed in the regular season, they were basically playoff-atmosphere games, because if we don't win those games, we don't get in."

The Cardinals' final regular-season win, a Saturday nail-biter over the Brewers, told Wainwright all he needed to know.

"We're down 2-0, and all of a sudden we're winning 3-2, and I had one single warm-up pitch," he recalled. "As soon as the three runs scored, they said, 'Adam, get up.' And that's when I knew that I was the guy. There was no way in the world I was going to let myself fail when I was thrown into a situation like that."

He'd been prepared for the moment not only by the coaching staff, but by pitchers who had been there. Isringhausen chose not to be threatened by the kid. He took him in, gave him tips, showed him how to tame the beast that is closing.

Looper, who had been signed in part to take over as closer when and if Isringhausen was no longer available, did the same for Wainwright. He acted as a teammate rather than a competitor. The two veterans, along with bullpen coach Marty Mason and the rest of the staff, looked out for Wainwright. They knew he had the stuff, and they would give him the education to use it.

"Those two guys helped me more than you'll ever know," Wainwright said. "I can almost guarantee I wouldn't have gotten through that [otherwise]. Marty Mason helped me a lot too. Marty will stand right by you and chirp in your ear and get you so fired up to go into a game you feel like you're a gladiator or something."

Each time Wainwright went to the mound to close a game, he felt more like a warrior. He felt more in control, more prepared and able to handle the task. And that was good, because each time, the stakes were higher.

After finishing off two essential wins in the season's final week,

Wainwright seized the closing job in the playoffs. No announcement was made, but none was needed. He recorded the final out of each of St. Louis' three wins in the National League Division Series against San Diego, pitching 3⅔ innings without allowing a run.

The youth and inexperience of the St. Louis bullpen, headed by Wainwright, became less of a story with each game. Wainwright and fellow rookies Josh Kinney and Tyler Johnson kept getting the call, and kept recording the biggest outs. The talent and effectiveness of the kiddie corps was what everyone talked about.

As he thrived in Isringhausen's job, though, Wainwright couldn't help thinking of the man whose spot he was taking. Isringhausen was nothing but a professional throughout, but everyone on the team knew it was killing him not to be a part of the Cardinals' October run. Wainwright certainly knew it.

"I felt bad for Izzy," he said. "He would probably tell me not to feel bad for him because he's been in a World Series before. But Izzy is a big part of our team. He's a huge part of our clubhouse. He keeps people in line, and he keeps it loose too. He's a guy that you look to for advice, a guy that you respect, a guy that's been through everything.

"I almost wanted it to be him. Almost."

Not that he had any plans to vacate his post. When the National League Championship Series started, Wainwright was already something of a phenomenon, drawing extensive media interest as a rookie closer on a playoff team. It was one of the few optimistic storylines about a Cardinals team that was an enormous underdog to the New York Mets.

The Mets cruised in Game 1, beating St. Louis 2-0, behind a brilliant Tom Glavine outing. They were in control again in Game 2 until St. Louis rallied against the New York bullpen. Wainwright got the final two outs of a 9-6 win at Shea Stadium. Though he didn't quite qualify for a save, he surely earned his money in the madhouse environment of Shea.

It was Game 3, though, that marked the Cardinals as contenders to win the series, with Jeff Suppan pitching eight brilliant innings. The five-run lead that the Redbirds took into the ninth inning was big enough that Wainwright wasn't needed—the Cards' first October

2006 win where Wainwright didn't get out No. 27.

A blowout loss in Game 4 evened the series, but six gutsy innings from Jeff Weaver gave St. Louis a lead going into the final frames of Game 5 at home. Wainwright got four outs for his second save and fifth game finished in the playoffs. The Cards were going back to New York with a chance to close it out and win an improbable pennant.

Actually, improbable didn't even cover it. It was shocking to see the league's best regular-season team—a club that rolled to 97 wins—in jeopardy against the 83-win Redbirds. Yet when ace Chris Carpenter couldn't deliver the Game 6 victory, everything seemed to turn 180 degrees. New York had a deciding Game 7 on its home turf, in front of its raucous fans. History favored the Mets, as well—it had been 31 years since any team lost Game 6 on the road and then bounced back to win Game 7 on the other guys' field. Eleven clubs had tried and failed.

This Game 7 was everything Game 7 is supposed to be. Both starting pitchers, Jeff Suppan and Oliver Perez, pitched beautifully. The Mets took a quick lead in the first, but the Cardinals tied it up in the next half-inning. And it got better from there.

In the sixth, the Cardinals came agonizingly close to taking a two-run lead. After Jim Edmonds' one-out walk, Scott Rolen crushed a high, deep fly ball to left field. But Endy Chavez made an absolutely spectacular snow-cone catch, reaching full extension and robbing a home run from Rolen. Chavez doubled Edmonds off of first, ending the inning and sending the Queens crowd into hysterics.

When the Mets mounted a threat in the next half-inning, everyone in the stadium was sure they were going to capitalize on the moment and roll to a win. Everyone except Suppan. With the bases loaded, the Cardinals starter struck out Jose Valentin, and got Chavez to fly out. It remains the unheralded turning point of a truly great game.

"They had every ounce of momentum going into the inning," Wainwright said. "After that catch, the whole crowd was just ignited. The whole team felt a certain energy. And Endy was coming up to bat also. So it was like, 'Jeez, are you kidding me?' It couldn't work out more of a storybook kind of ending than that. They had everything in their favor, and Suppan just kind of said, 'The heck with that, I'm getting out of this.'"

Tension reigned over the next two innings as the score remained tied. Yadier Molina took Aaron Heilman deep in the top of the ninth, and suddenly the underdog Cardinals were three outs away from the World Series. Shea went as quiet as 50,000 New Yorkers can get, while the Cardinals dugout and bullpen erupted.

It meant celebration time to just about everyone in a gray uniform. But for Wainwright, there was no time to celebrate. Molina's blast meant only one thing: time to get to work. He began warming up in the visitors bullpen at Shea Stadium, getting ready for the biggest and toughest three outs of his life.

"Everybody's going crazy in the stands and all of a sudden a huge hush comes over them," Wainwright said. "Everybody in Shea Stadium got the wind knocked out of them. Our bullpen is going crazy. And yet, I'm staying focused because I know I'm the guy. So all I do is, I turn and I walk right to the mound. That's a good feeling to have. Knowing that the biggest situation in your life is about to happen and you're the man to do it."

He'd been preparing his whole life for this assignment, whether he had realized it or not.

Wainwright strode to the mound and prepared to face Valentin. He fell behind Valentin in the count, eventually giving up a bleeder single at 3-2. Chavez also got ahead of Wainwright and singled, bringing the winning run to the plate with nobody out.

A right-hander and a left-hander began warming up in the Cardinals bullpen. Duncan came out for a conference with Wainwright, Molina, and Rolen. Wainwright had gotten in trouble before he even realized what was going on. Now it was his job to get out.

"I was so amped up, so geared up, that I couldn't control where I was throwing the ball or my emotions," Wainwright said. "The first two guys got hits, but that is what allowed me to get through that inning. When they got on base, I said, 'The heck with that. This is not how I pitch. I'm focusing. Let's just get back to my game. They're not scoring.'"

He got ahead of pinch hitter Cliff Floyd with a fastball, working another difficult at-bat before Floyd watched a curveball for strike three. One down, but damage coming: the Mets order turned over, bringing up Jose Reyes, the dangerous and speedy leadoff man. But Reyes lined out to center field for the second out. He struck the ball well, but Jim Edmonds tracked it, and the Cardinals were one out away.

Now it was Wainwright versus catcher Paul Lo Duca, two outs, two on, and everything on the line. And if Lo Duca wasn't threat enough, someone else was lurking—Cardinal-killer Carlos Beltran stood on deck. Beltran had almost single-handedly beaten the Cards in 2004, when St. Louis held off a furious fight from the Astros in the NLCS. Yet Wainwright did the one thing he didn't want to do. He walked Lo Duca, bringing up Beltran.

The switch-hitting slugger strode toward the plate, and Wainwright and Molina conferenced. This time Duncan remained in the dugout and Rolen remained at third. It was not a matter of cooling Wainwright down. It was all about the immediate task at hand— getting Beltran out.

"Yadi came to the mound and we originally decided to go sinker away," Wainwright said. "But the thing about Beltran is, if you make an ounce of a mistake, he's going to hurt you. The first ball there, I've got to think that he's going to be aggressive. So if I miss location with a sinker, hopefully I miss out of the zone, but if I miss in the zone, he's going to kill it. He's going to really hurt that ball."

So even after agreeing on a fastball, both Wainwright and Molina had a change of heart. It led to what may have been the most important pitch of the at-bat, though surely not the most famous.

"Immediately he [Molina] ran back to home plate and started tapping his chest," Wainwright said. "And I knew we were doing something different. And I was hoping it was going to be a change-up, and it was.

"If I throw a changeup and it's in the zone, in that situation there, there's no possible way that he can look for that pitch. None. So even if he does swing at it and I miss in the zone, I've got a good chance of having him off-balance."

Beltran took the first-pitch changeup. In terms of location, it was an eminently hittable pitch—over the plate and up a little bit. In terms of selection, it was anything but.

"It was a perfect call," said Wainwright. "Because from then on, he's like, 'Man, this guy has no idea what he's doing out here. I don't know what's coming.' He had no idea how to approach me after that, I don't think."

Even the television broadcast crew was mystified. Analyst Tim McCarver referred to the pitch as a fastball. Baseball's old law says you don't throw a first pitch changeup, because after all, what are you changing from? But that's exactly why the pitch worked so well.

"A changeup is designed to be a pitch that's swung at, a pitch that's put in play," Wainwright said. "I threw that with the intention that he was going to pop it up to second or roll over that ball. A taken strike wasn't exactly what I had in mind for that, but it worked out just as well."

At 0-1, Wainwright broke off a curveball, but he missed his spot. With Molina set up outside, Wainwright left the ball too far inside. But the pitch had so much movement on it that all Beltran could do was foul it off. Oh-and-two. Beltran had seen the curveball, and flailed at it. All he had to show was a bruised right ankle, as the foul grazed him on its way down.

Well ahead in the count, Molina and Wainwright both knew a strike wasn't necessary. What they needed was a pitch Beltran would chase out of the zone. Sometimes this plan is called "wasting a pitch," but that's not an accurate depiction. It's more like trying to get the batter to waste a swing. The hitter must defend the plate with an 0-2 count, so maybe he'll defend the area beyond the plate also.

A big-breaking curveball like Wainwright's is the perfect offering for an 0-2 count, even against a selective hitter like Beltran. After Molina gave Wainwright the signal, he put his mitt almost on the ground. Bury this one. Better to miss in the dirt than in the strike zone. Molina had confidence that Wainwright would not hang the pitch. Wainwright had confidence that if he did bounce the ball, Molina would be all over it, and the runners would not advance. Everybody was on the same page.

Wainwright was set for the biggest pitch of his life.

And he made an absolutely brilliant pitch, a curveball that started way up high and dropped way down low. It was the very definition of how a curveball should look, the kind of thing you might put on an instructional video—except that it would be unfair to ask anyone else to duplicate a pitch like that. It completely befuddled Beltran, who stood as though he'd never seen any curveball before, much less one that good. The Mets outfielder was so baffled that despite the 0-2 count, despite the runners on base, despite the chance to drive in pennant-winning runs, Beltran just froze. He took the pitch.

And rookie Adam Wainwright was suddenly an October hero. Beltran was not a goat, because no one could have hit that pitch, and no one could be blamed for taking it. It wasn't that Beltran lost the battle. Wainwright won it.

"Not one time in that inning did I think about losing," Wainwright recalled. "I didn't think about [Beltran] getting a hit. I didn't think about Reyes getting a hit. I didn't think about Cliff Floyd getting a hit. It just never crossed my mind. And I think if it had crossed my mind, if I would have started really worrying about, 'Oh, this guy's a Cardinal killer,' he probably would have killed me. But since I didn't, I had the upper hand."

A gray-clad mob descended upon Wainwright. The Cardinals had won one of the great playoff games in history, and they'd closed it out with the kid on the mound. Eight days later, St. Louis won its first World Series championship in 25 years. Again, Wainwright was on the mound for the final out. Showing his remarkable repertoire, he fanned Brandon Inge on three sliders to end the Fall Classic. Not a curveball in the bunch.

Eight and a half months after his journey began, Wainwright earned the thing that all ballplayers only dare to dream about—a World Series ring. But when he looks back, it's Game 7 that he remembers.

"I definitely get more comments about that than anything else," he said. "I never hear anything about the World Series. It's all, 'Man, that pitch to Beltran.'"

Wainwright still hears it from Mets fans when he goes back to New York. When an out-of-contention St. Louis team made a one-game swing to Queens in September of 2007, New York partisans greeted him with taunts about his club's struggles. They pointed out—not in so many words—that in October of '07 the right-hander would be golfing instead of pitching.

But Wainwright had the perfect comeback. And he'll always have it in his back pocket.

"One guy says, 'Hey Wainwright! You're not going to be striking out Beltran in Game 7 this year!'" he recalls.

"I said, 'Hey, I've only got to do it once.'"

CHAPTER 2

GLENN BRUMMER

"Brummer's stealing home!"

Cardinals broadcaster Mike Shannon made the call not so much out of excitement, but disbelief. Glenn Brummer? Stealing *any* base, let alone home plate in the 12th inning?

Yes, yes, and yes. Brummer, a second-year player appearing in the 50th game of his major league career, was the unlikeliest hero for the Cardinals in 1982. At 27, he wasn't a prospect but already something of a journeyman. He was one of three catchers on the roster, along with star Darrell Porter and old sage Gene Tenace, and his appearance in the game at all wasn't a certainty that day.

Doubly unlikely was that Brummer, a catcher, would make his name for a base-running play. Speed was not exactly his calling card. Yet Brummer stole home in the literal heat of St. Louis in August, not to mention the figurative heat of the pennant race. He took the chance, and he made it. And in so doing, he burned his name into the memories of Cardinals fans all over the Midwest and the country.

On August 22, 1982, Glenn Brummer became a household name in Cardinal Nation. His hometown hero status was cemented two months later when that Cardinals team won the franchise's first World Series championship in 15 years.

"It just kind of put a little spark in that team," Brummer said. "You had the feeling, 'Hey, we're going to win it.' If we can win like that . . . We did have a good team. Defense, speed, good pitching. It was just a little spark. It was just a little spark to drive us on. We said,

'Hey, we do have a chance of winning.'"

When you talk about the 1982 Cardinals, you talk about Hall of Famers Bruce Sutter and Ozzie Smith, of course. Soon the conversation will turn to Keith Hernandez, Joaquin Andujar, Bob Forsch, and manager Whitey Herzog. But invariably, Brummer's name comes up. Sometimes it comes up before anyone else's, even though Brummer got a grand total of 64 at-bats that year, and none in the postseason. He is associated with that team as strongly as players who had 10 times the at-bats. Everyone remembers where they were when Brummer stole home, and Brummer himself revisits the play every day.

"It's amazing that just one play really made my career," Brummer marveled. "One play that lasted about three seconds. It's amazing how people remember me stealing home. I'm in awe of what's gone on and how many people remember.

"I went to a signing, and this one old-timer, he was about 70 years old, he said, 'I remember when I was a kid and Pearl Harbor was bombed. I remember when JFK was assassinated. And I remember where I was when Glenn Brummer stole home.' That's all he said. That's something else."

Sometimes unlikely heroes grow weary of the spotlight. Sometimes they become offended or feel slighted. They want to point to the other things that make them special. Don't define me by one moment, they insist.

Not Brummer. He still revels in his one moment. He still treasures his taste of baseball immortality, the brightest spot in a brief career.

Brummer played in 178 major league games. He took all of 347 at-bats, hit exactly one big-league homer and was thrown out in eight of his 12 steal attempts. And no one cares about any of those numbers. They care about Brummer stealing home.

"I think about it every day," he said, "but I didn't think it would be this big. Why is it a big play? I don't know. Has it ever happened before? Is it going to happen again? It's obvious that it doesn't happen

Glenn Brummer was the very definition of a role player, yet his name became a household name thanks to one play on one hot afternoon. *Brace Photos*

every day. People have asked me, has it ever happened? I say I don't know. A walk-off steal, it doesn't happen every game."

The Cardinals started play on Sunday, August 22, with a two-game lead over the Phillies in the National League East division. They'd been in first place for only a few weeks, and a young team was trying to end the franchise's 14-year postseason drought. Philadelphia had been to the playoffs in each of the previous two years, and the Phils were keeping the pressure on the Redbirds.

The San Francisco Giants, clinging to contention five games behind the Braves in the National League West, were in town for the rubber game of a three-game series. It was, of course, hot. Casey Stengel once joked of Busch Stadium, "It holds the heat well."

The Cardinals took an early 3-0 lead, but San Francisco got all those runs, and one more, back in the sixth. The Giants still led, 4-3, in the ninth inning, and it took a minor miracle for the game to even go into extra innings. Ken Oberkfell hit a two-out RBI double in the ninth to tie the score, and on the contest went. And on and on. The two clubs had been playing for four hours when Brummer broke for home.

Brummer had actually entered the game as a pinch runner. Steve Braun pinch hit for Gene Tenace in the eighth, and Brummer came in to run for Braun. It was not exactly speed for speed, but Brummer obviously turned out to be the sage choice for a runner. Actually, he just happened to be the remaining option to catch, since Porter was set to pinch hit. Brummer remained in the game as the catcher, and he struck out in the 10th inning.

In the 12th though, Brummer stroked a one-out single off of lefty Gary Lavelle. Willie McGee followed with a single, sending Brummer to second—again, be reminded that the man was not exactly a speed demon. Julio Gonzalez's popup provided the second out, and Smith reached on an infield single.

So it comes to every kid's backyard dream—two outs, bases loaded, extra innings. But it's all set up for batter David Green, not Brummer, to be the hero. Green had already singled and reached base as a hit batsman in the game, and scored on Oberkfell's game-tying double. Brummer was the furthest thing from the minds of nearly everyone—including Giants third baseman Darrell Evans and pitcher Lavelle. That just set Brummer's wheels turning.

"Lavelle was pitching out of the stretch," Brummer recalls. "He's got his back to me. And most left-handers won't check the runner on third if they're pitching out of the stretch. If they're pitching out of the windup, they'll glance at you, but they can't do nothing.

"In this particular case, Lavelle, a tall left-hander, had a high leg kick and he was slow to home. And he was pitching out of the stretch. The third baseman, a lot of times, tries to hold the runner close. But Darrell Evans was playing off the bag and deep, toward left field. And rightly so, because all they need is an out. So they ain't going to pay no attention to me. They're going to try to get the hitter.

"That's their thought process—get the hitter, get back in the dugout, and play some more baseball. They're not even thinking of the base runner, of anybody taking off. That was my thought process. His back's to me, so no one really cares about where I'm at."

Brummer actually wanted to go one pitch earlier than he did. But the play was so audacious that third-base coach Chuck Hiller first put the kibosh on it.

"For the first couple or three pitches, we're waiting for David Green to get a base hit and win the game," Brummer said. "But the count went to 2-1, and I turned around and looked at Chuck Hiller and said, 'You know I can go.' And he nodded and said, 'I know.'

"'Should I?'

"'Well, better not.'

"But I didn't listen to him. The next pitch was a strike, so that made it 2-2. I had wanted to go on 2-1. I could have gone any time, but 2-1, I really did want to go. I wanted to go on that pitch, but Chuck said, better not. And the next pitch was a strike, so that made it 2-2. I really didn't want to go on two strikes. But the play was there and everything was right, so it was just a matter of hopefully it wasn't going to be strike three."

It wasn't. Or if it was, home plate umpire Dave Pallone didn't call it. Lavelle went into his delivery, and Brummer broke for home. Green, a right-handed hitter, started to move once he saw Brummer coming, though he wasn't actually in on the play from the start.

"David Green had a feel for me, and he stepped out," Brummer said. "But I was going anyway. I wasn't stopping. I didn't know what David Green was going to do, but I was going."

Catcher Milt May lunged forward to catch the ball as early as pos-

sible and try to put a tag on Brummer. Pallone, as surprised as anyone, found his attention diverted to the developing play, rather than
the pitch. The ball may well have been right down the pipe. It may
have been a foot out of the zone.

Pallone simply called the play at the plate, and he called
Brummer safe. Shannon made his famous, simple call, and fans all
over KMOX's mammoth broadcasting range were stunned. Even the
people at the ballpark still weren't exactly sure what had happened—
Brummer included.

"I said to [Shannon], 'You saw the play better than I did. What
happened?'

"Mike's still watching, I'm in the dugout, and after the play happened, Mike's still wondering what's going on. He said [Giants man-
ager] Frank Robinson stayed out there for 10, 12, 15 minutes wondering what the pitch was, if it was strike three. Meanwhile, Whitey's
got the grounds crew on the field, rolling that tarp out. It's done.
Ballgame. Whitey said, 'Let's get out of here. Let's try to get people
off.'

"I'm sure there was a standing O, but I had no idea what was
going on. I should have tipped my hat, but I didn't know what was
going on. I just went in the clubhouse and had a cold beer. I did not
know Frank Robinson was out there for that long."

What if Brummer had been wrong? What if this second-year,
backup catcher, not at all established, had been out? He had gone
against the suggestion of his coach, and made a highly risky play. The
consequences might have been dire, but the thought never crossed
Brummer's mind. He wasn't worried about the downside, because he
saw no downside from his perspective. Brummer saw no circumstance in which he was going to be out. At worst, Green would strike
out, or would somehow put the ball in play. Brummer was certain,
and remains certain, that there was no way he would be tagged out.

"When I took off, I knew I was going to be there, but I didn't
know what was going to happen," he said. "I knew I would be safe.
But was David Green going to hit the ball? I beat the ball there. Was
Milt May going to catch it? Drop it? I don't know. Maybe a balk
would be called, but if he didn't see me, he wasn't going to balk.

"On the replay, Lavelle did not see me go. He threw the ball right
down the middle. To be honest with you, it was strike three right

down the middle. David Green stepped out, so he's not going to hit it. Dave Pallone, the umpire, stepped away from the play, so he's not going to call the pitch. So Milt May, he probably did the right thing. He went out front and caught the ball and made the tag. But I was underneath the tag, so that was it. Ballgame."

And Brummer became one of the best-known names in the long history of the Cardinals. Mike Ramsey, Dane Iorg, Green, and Gonzalez all saw more at-bats and more games than Brummer that season. But none is remembered like the Olney, Illinois native.

The run gave the Cardinals a pivotal playoff-chase win, and dealt a painful loss to the also-contending Giants. St. Louis eventually won the National League East by three games, but the lead was as small as a half-game in mid-September. There was never any doubt that Brummer's play was a big part of the Redbirds' run to glory.

If Brummer didn't know that himself, right away, he realized it quickly. He was literally an overnight sensation—his teammates and his fellow St. Louisans let him know what he'd accomplished in a variety of ways, starting the following morning.

"They had the newspaper sitting on my stool the next day," Brummer said. "I couldn't buy a newspaper! I went out to try to buy a newspaper, to see what was in it, and I couldn't buy one. That afternoon, somebody brought one and put a bottle of champagne on my stool in the locker room. Jim Kaat got everybody to sign home plate, and Amadee, the artist, drew me a picture. They signed it and everything, gave me home plate."

It was one of very few champagne-awarding kind of days in Brummer's career. He popped the corks with the Cardinals three times in '82, when they won the division, the League Championship Series, and the World Series, and he made a brief appearance on the field at the end of the Cards' blowout Game 6 World Series win. But never again was he the center of attention, the center of everything, like he was on August 22, 1982.

"After I stole home, which was a career highlight, then playing in Game 6 of the World Series and winning in Game 7, I kept on playing, but I could have ended it right there, with those two things. But I kept on playing. I went on and played with the Cardinals in '83 and '84, and then in '85, the Cardinals released me in Spring Training. And Whitey turned around and got me another job with the Texas

Rangers for another year in the big leagues. So I got into my pension then, which helps nowadays.

"But yeah, after winning the World Series, that was pretty much it as far as highlights in my career."

Brummer chased the dream for a while longer after his last game in the big leagues. He played for the Pirates' Triple-A affiliate in Hawaii, and he tried to make the rival Cubs as a backup catcher. He ended up as Chicago's bullpen catcher for a spell before heading south. He served as a catching instructor and Spring Training coach in the Phillies organization, living in Florida for nearly two decades after he hung it up as a player.

Whether he was working with players in the spring or traveling as a roving catching instructor, he always ran into people who knew his name. And his play. It's almost as though his name has some extra words—"Glenn Brummer, the guy who stole home," instead of simply Glenn Brummer.

"I was in Martinsville, Virginia, coaching rookie ball," he recalls. "This guy came out of nowhere when I was sitting in the bullpen. He goes, 'Brummer! I remember when you stole home!' I mean, we're in no-man's-land. 'I was there!' It's amazing. All over the United States, where as a coach and an instructor I've traveled, everywhere, I go to ballparks, and people come out of nowhere. When they announce me as a coach or an instructor at the game, they come down and say, 'Hey, Brummer, I was there at that game.'"

If 47,000 people were actually at Busch Stadium that day, surely 147,000 or more claim to have been there. More than 40,000 were in attendance 25 years later, when Brummer threw out a ceremonial first pitch at new Busch Stadium on the anniversary of the play. He was still a star, even with the '07 team in the hunt for a championship of its own.

"That's one chance in a lifetime—unless they do it on the 50th anniversary," he quipped. "But I might not be around."

Even the people who weren't there recall it vividly.

"A lot of them are pretty honest with me," Brummer said. "They just say, 'Hey, I remember the play, but I wasn't there.' A lot of them say, 'I was there and I seen it.'

"A lot of them heard it over the radio. In fact, one guy came up to me and he said, 'I was driving on the interstate toward Springfield,

Illinois, Interstate 55, and I ran off the road.' A guy said he was flipping burgers and hot dogs on his grill and when he heard the play, he upset the grill. But this one guy said, 'I ran off the road. I parked it and had to get myself together.'"

That's what the Cardinals mean in St. Louis. And that's a big part of why Brummer packed up after a healthy stint in Florida and moved back to the St. Louis area. He's a hometown boy and he wanted to be among his people. Just like so many people who grew up following the Cardinals, Brummer never stopped checking the box scores. Even when he was working in other organizations, his love was for the team he knew best.

"I was always following the Cardinals," he said. "Every day I'd go into the box scores and look at the Cardinals and see how they were doing. I've been a Cardinals fan even when I was a kid. I got to go to Sportsman's Park and watch a game, back in 1960 or '61. I got to see Stan Musial play, Willie Mays, some of the great players. My dad, Bob Brummer, even had a year in the minor leagues with the Cardinals."

So people seek him out more these days. He's recognized more often, both by name and by face. But for Brummer, it's not a burden. It's 100 percent the opposite. He marvels at it.

"I do at times," he said. "Right after I threw out the first pitch, they had a place to sit down and eat inside the club area, and people just talked about the play. One play they remember is Brummer stealing home, and that was 25 years ago. Some of them must have been five or six years old at the time. And then there's the people who are my age, and they go crazy over it."

Had Brummer achieved his moment of fame in another city, he'd still be remembered, of course. If he had stolen home for the Giants, or the White Sox, or the Braves, surely people would still know his name in San Francisco or Chicago or Atlanta.

But it wouldn't mean the same thing to the fans, because Cardinals baseball has a unique pull. And it wouldn't mean the same to Brummer. Having his moment at home made it all the more memorable. And it still makes his homecoming sweet. Brummer is happy to admit that the play is part of why he's back in St. Louis.

"That's special. That was one of the reasons why I came back to this area from down in Florida. I wanted to relate to more people. I came back to enjoy the moment, enjoy my life, spend it with the Cardinal fans. It's very special to me. That's one of the reasons I did come back here, to listen to people's responses. Because they're still responding to it."

And they will, for as long as Brummer is around.

CHAPTER 3

TOM PAGNOZZI

For most of his career, Tom Pagnozzi's timing just wasn't quite right. Pagnozzi was late arriving in the major leagues, slowed by a series of wrist injuries that kept him in the bus leagues for an extra year or more. He was late getting to the Cardinals, joining St. Louis at the tail end of a mini-dynasty before enduring a frustrating fruitless stretch.

But if he sometimes had bad luck with the "when" of playing baseball, he was dead on as far as the "where." The three-time Gold Glover, who grew up in Arizona as a Dodgers fan, found a home quickly in the south-central United States. He attended the University of Arkansas, and settled in northwest Arkansas. He still lives in the area, 25 years after his college days ended.

And when Pagnozzi arrived in the big leagues, he again ended up in just the right place. He played 12 seasons, all as a Cardinal, beginning and ending his career with the same franchise. He still identifies with St. Louis, still watches the Redbirds play, still attends team events. He even has a nephew, Matt, playing in the organization.

"I wasn't a great player," Pagnozzi admits. "I was a good player. And I was very fortunate [to stay in one place], especially with the St. Louis Cardinals, because . . . what a great organization. If you talk about organizations, you've got the Yankees, the Dodgers, the Cardinals—not even Boston. Until recently, they didn't win. It was those three teams that were constantly in it. You hit some dry stretches, but they did it.

"To say that I played for one of them my whole career, being just a good player, it's remarkable. It's a great town. They love their baseball. They understand their baseball. The neat thing about them is that, when the opponent made a great play, they recognized it. It wasn't like that in every city."

Pagnozzi grew more and more fond of St. Louis the longer he played there, but it's safe to say that he was hooked from the very beginning.

That's because his second game appearance in the big leagues came in one of the most famous contests in team history—the "Seat Cushion Game," which was capped by a Tom Herr grand slam. Three batters before Herr's famous walk-off slam, Pagnozzi picked up his first major-league base hit, driving in the game's tying run. The homer stands as Herr's signature accomplishment in a distinguished Cardinals career. But it's Pagnozzi, not Herr, who still has manager Whitey Herzog's lineup card from April 18, 1987.

Five days earlier, Pagnozzi made his big-league debut. He caught the last three innings of a game in Pittsburgh after starting catcher Steve Lake was removed for a pinch hitter. He sat for the next four games, until the Mets came to town for a weekend series.

In the mid-to-late 1980s, National League matchups didn't get much better than Mets-Cardinals. The two teams alternated National League East titles from '85 through '88, and twice they finished 1-2. The players loved competing against each other, and the fans may have loved it even more.

"To say [there was] a team you dislike, that was probably the team," Pagnozzi said. "Because they were the media darlings, New York, and our fans loved to hate New York. They had a great team. So it was a great thing for the fans. They loved to hate them.

"You loved going in and playing rivalry games. Not only is it exciting to the fans, but to guys that are consumed by the game and have such a passion for the game, they love those. I loved going into Wrigley Field because of the old field. I have a passion for the game.

The "Seat Cushion Game" may be best known for Tom Herr's heroics, but it's Tom Pagnozzi who has the lineup card from that night. *Brace Photos*

I love it. I watch every game now. I'm consumed by it. Not every player is like that."

When the rivals met head to head for the first time in '87, the fans at Busch Stadium got their money's worth. The Cardinals won the Friday night game, 4-3, a battle with three lead changes. Saturday brought the "seat cushion game," and on Sunday the Redbirds took an early lead and held on for a 4-2 win.

"I was hoping it was like that every day," Pagnozzi said. "There are certain games that are so much more fun to play in. A 10-2 game, hell, you win and it's over. I'd rather play 162 of those games. I don't know if our bodies could handle it or our minds could handle it, but that's when it's the most fun."

So although Pagnozzi would rather have reached the big leagues sooner, his early games were worth the wait. It was quite a frustrating wait, though.

He was drafted in 1983, an eighth-round pick out of Arkansas. Pagnozzi made his way through the minors on the strength of his bat, a contrast to his three Gold Glove major league career.

By '85, Pagnozzi was a promising and rising prospect in the Cardinals system. He began the year at Double-A Arkansas and made it to Triple-A Louisville. He had a solid campaign in winter ball, but broke his wrist playing over the winter. Yet Pagnozzi recovered for a strong start in '86 before another wrist injury derailed him.

"They had a policy then, since we only had one trainer," Pagnozzi remembers. "If you got hurt, you waited until after the game and you went to the hospital. And I remember [manager Jim Fregosi] telling the trainer, Hap Hudson, 'Take him, get that straight right now.' I said, 'Oh, I can wait till after the game.' He said, 'No, go now.' I came back with a cast and he was like, 'You don't know what this cost you.' I said, 'What?' He goes, 'After the game, come see me.'"

Fregosi told Pagnozzi that the Cardinals had been looking to trade starting catcher Mike Heath, who was struggling badly. Heath didn't even get his batting average over .100 until the second week in May.

The Cardinals did later trade Heath to Detroit. Had Pagnozzi been healthy, his path would have been clear. But not only was he not healthy, he actually got hurt yet again, breaking the same wrist a third time as he tried to return to action. Thus, when Pagnozzi went to

Spring Training in 1987, he knew the odds were against him.

"I go to winter ball, then I go to camp knowing that I'm going to go to Triple-A," he said. "I missed all of the year before. I was just learning to catch. I had some defensive problems. I wasn't very good defensively, which is kind of funny when I go on to win three Gold Gloves. But I came up more as a hitter. That's what was keeping me out of the big leagues, was the ability to catch."

If Pagnozzi wasn't sure of his place at the start of Spring Training, the Cardinals did something at the end of camp that made it entirely evident. On April 1, six days before Opening Day, they traded for four-time All-Star Tony Peña. Pagnozzi's ticket was punched.

But then again, maybe it wasn't. In Peña's third game in a St. Louis uniform, he was hit by a pitch and broke his thumb. The call went to Louisville, and this time Pagnozzi was able to take advantage of a chance. He'd been in the big leagues for less than a week when the Mets came to town. After the tense opener, the Saturday matchup featured nearly four hours of absolute insanity.

New York charged to a 5-0 lead, chasing Danny Cox after three innings. In the bottom of the fourth, St. Louis got all five runs back, thanks to five singles, a double, and two walks. And the wildness was just starting.

Herr doubled in the sixth, scoring Ozzie Smith and putting the Cardinals ahead, 6-5. Each team went 1-2-3 in the seventh, and after a leadoff Mets single in the eighth, manager Whitey Herzog called on Todd Worrell. The Cards closer got Kevin McReynolds to fly out, and Darryl Strawberry was caught stealing, but Worrell walked the bases loaded before escaping with the one-run lead still intact.

The Cardinals couldn't add on in the bottom of the eighth, and in the ninth, New York took the lead. Worrell handed out two more walks before he was finally removed for Bill Dawley. McReynolds and Howard Johnson rapped back-to-back two-out RBI singles against Dawley, and the Cardinals trailed for the first time since the fourth.

So of course they came back. Smith led off the ninth with a walk. Herr sacrificed him to second. And with Jack Clark at the plate, the future Hall of Famer stole third base and came home to score on a throwing error by another Cooperstown-bound player: catcher Gary Carter. Clark struck out, and so did McGee—this April classic was bound for extra innings. And a young catcher was getting ready for his first major league pinch-hit appearance.

"That was the most incredible part about Whitey Herzog," Pagnozzi said. "Whitey had a thing, especially with the younger players. What he was really good at was communicating with us. He'd come down in the seventh inning and go, 'Pags, if so-and-so is in there in the ninth against so-and-so, you're hitting.' It's not that we weren't in the game, but as a younger player it helps you focus a little bit better."

Herzog gave Pagnozzi a heads-up, and the rookie started getting serious about his preparations. Meanwhile, the Cardinals bullpen continued to struggle with command. Al Pedrique drew a leadoff walk in the 10th, and Dave Magadan bunted him over. A Lenny Dykstra grounder sent Pedrique to third, and the light-hitting infielder scored on a Dave LaPoint wild pitch. Once again, the Mets led. Once again, the Cardinals were in danger of watching all their efforts go to waste. Luckily, St. Louis escaped without further damage, giving the home team three outs to score a run.

It scored five.

Lefty Jesse Orosco, who pitched the ninth, got the first batter when Tito Landrum grounded out. Terry Pendleton singled, as did catcher Steve Lake, and the Cardinals had runners on first and second—the tying run in scoring position and the winning run on base. Curt Ford's spot in the batting order came up, and Herzog called on right-handed Pagnozzi to face the lefty Orosco. It was the first career pinch-hitting appearance for Pagnozzi. Then again, it was the second plate appearance of any kind.

Pagnozzi remembers having a spring in his step as he walked to the dish, but no fear.

"It's a nervousness, it's an excitement," he said. "First of all, it was really my first big at-bat in the major leagues. Tight game, back and forth, fans crazy, New York Mets—yeah, I was nervous and excited and just looking for a pitch. I knew he was going to keep the ball away from me, and I just wanted to go that way with it off of Orosco. Just hit it the other way—that was kind of the way I liked to hit the ball anyway—and just hit it hard. I can't control where it goes. And good things happened."

Pagnozzi saw the pitch on the outside part of the plate, stayed with it and poked it to the opposite field for a game-tying RBI single.

Pendleton scored and pinch runner Tom Lawless advanced to second. And the Cardinals got their first hint of what was to come a few minutes later, as a few seat cushions made their way from the stands onto the field. The game was briefly delayed, and when action resumed, Vince Coleman grounded out. That advanced the runners, and Smith walked to load the bases.

Up came Herr, who drove in his share of runs but was never a power threat. The St. Louis second baseman amassed 110 RBIs in 1985, but hit only eight home runs. When '87 was over, he'd gone deep twice but collected 83 ribbies. Herr was far from a typical No. 3 hitter, but on a good day he could be dangerous.

This was a good day. Herr took Orosco deep. Ballgame. Chaos at Busch Stadium.

"I thought when he hit it, it was gone," Pagnozzi said. "I really did. From where I was, I thought it was gone. But prior to that, I was just thinking, 'Get to third base. Touch third. On a single, you've got to touch the base.' When he hit it, I just remember taking off and looking at Tommy Herr, and his hands were up in the air, and I knew it was gone at that point."

Seat cushions pelted the field as the Cardinals celebrated. On the KMOX broadcast, Jack Buck quipped that they'd be holding seat cushion night again on Sunday, because every seat cushion had been thrown back.

Tom Herr was a hero, and Tom Pagnozzi had a night he would never forget.

"Everybody was patting [Herr] on the back, jumping on him," Pagnozzi said. "The amazing thing about this sport is that at moments like that, we all become kids again. You see a big play, a big hit, where else do you see guys hugging each other and patting each other on the ass and jumping up and down?

"Regardless of if it's early in the season, winning games like that is still exciting. It still brings out that little boy in you like it was a sandlot game and someone hit a home run to win it. That's the amazing thing of the game. We're all from different places and we're teammates, and it's an incredible feeling."

It wasn't the last time Pagnozzi would enjoy an "incredible feeling" that weekend. The next day, in the series finale, he got his first big-league start behind the plate, and hit his first home run. He led off the fifth inning with a shot off Sid Fernandez, a 16-game winner the year before. He also threw out speedster Mookie Wilson trying to steal, and drew his first intentional walk.

"That first weekend," he said, "was a big weekend."

Pagnozzi enjoyed big-league meal money for another month after that while Peña healed. He went 7-for-33 (.212) over his first stint in the show, including his first grand slam on May 17 against the Reds. But on May 22, Peña came off the disabled list, and it was back to Louisville for Pagnozzi. He'd made an impression, though.

"I went back to Triple-A with the goal of needing to get ready," he said. "And it was funny, because when I was leaving, when Whitey sent me down in Houston, he looked at me and he goes, 'You did a great job for six weeks.' We were in first place when I left. And he goes, 'You will be back for the playoffs.'

"And I'm kind of like, 'OK, how much stock do you put in that?' I'm going to be back for the playoffs? I knew I had to go down to Triple-A and I had to play well. Because if you don't play well, it doesn't matter. But I expected to be called up September 1—not prior."

As is often the case, though, the manager was right. Pagnozzi spent three months in Triple-A before receiving an August 22 recall. Not only was he back before the playoffs, he was back before roster expansion. He was definitely on the team's radar.

Pagnozzi played little and hit less during his second tour in St. Louis, going 2-for-15 over the season's final six weeks. He made the playoff roster, though, and capped off a memorable rookie year with appearances in the National League Championship Series and the World Series.

"We played 71 games in a row in Triple-A, and on our off day, [manager] Mike Jorgensen knocks on my door," Pagnozzi remembers. "It's August 22 and he says, 'You need to be in Cincinnati by six o'clock tonight.' I looked at my wife and said goodbye. I headed to Cincinnati."

From that point on, Pagnozzi was pretty well established as a big leaguer. Unfortunately, that bad-timing bug bit again. As Pagnozzi's career waxed, the Cardinals' fortunes waned. The familiar names from the '80s dynasty moved on, one at a time.

Herr, Clark, John Tudor, and Bob Forsch were gone within a year after the '87 World Series loss. McGee played only 58 games in 1989 and was traded in '90. The culture changed, and so did the standards. The Redbirds finished in fifth in 1988, third in '89 and dead last in the National League East in '90. Over eight seasons from 1988-95, only once did the club even finish as high as second place.

"They won in '82, they lost in '85 and we lost in '87—I'm not calling it a dynasty, but August [Busch] Jr. was still alive and he loved baseball, and when he was around, we always knew that we had a chance. Then he died in '89, and things slowly changed after that. We were now a budget team.

"Whitey had left, and Joe Torre had come in. It wasn't really fair; people thought Joe couldn't manage. We had a losing record by a few games, we were right at .500 in his time. But if you look at what he was given—our pitching staff was depleted, we didn't have any stars outside of Ozzie. He was our star. We didn't have star power outside of the birds on the bat being on our chest."

Pagnozzi remained a good soldier, though, a bright spot on some bad teams. He made an All-Star Game in 1992 and had productive years at the plate in '94 and '96. He won Gold Gloves in '91, '92 and '94, becoming the first Cardinals backstop to bring home a Gold Glove.

And finally, in 1996, his patience was rewarded. The Cardinals returned to the postseason. They won the National League Central and swept the Padres in the Division Series. The season ended with the heartbreak of a seven-game loss to the Braves in the NLCS, but the foundation for a new Cardinal glory era had been laid.

Pagnozzi was one of the few links, along with Smith, one of the few men who played October games in St. Louis under both Herzog and Tony La Russa. Maybe his timing wasn't so bad after all.

"Growing up in Tucson, I was a huge Dodger fan," Pagnozzi said. "And if you look at the Dodgers, they had players that were there for a long time. When I was growing up, it was [Steve] Garvey at first, [Davey] Lopes at second, [Bill] Russell at short, Ron Cey at third. [Steve] Yeager and [Joe] Ferguson catching. All those guys played there a long time, and I thought that's the way it was when I was growing up.

"And then as you get older, you realize that guys change teams a lot more. It was very unusual for me—I wasn't a great player, I was a good player—to be able to stay there for 12 years and watch all those other guys bounce around."

CHAPTER 4

BOB FORSCH

The Cardinals organization embraces its history like few others in baseball. The team's Hall of Famers are always present—attending Opening Day, helping out in Spring Training, participating in community projects, and basically doing whatever is needed. The greats from the past are always willing to lend a hand, and they're always invited.

That can be inspiring to current players. After all, who couldn't use a pitching lesson from Bob Gibson or a pat on the back from Lou Brock? But it can also be a weight on their backs. When the team falls on hard times, the history can feel like a burden. Manager Tony La Russa has said that until he won a World Series ring in St. Louis, he wasn't really part of "the club."

Red Schoendienst, with two rings as a player and one as a manager, is in the club. Stan Musial, with three rings, is in the club. Gibson and Brock—with two apiece—are in the club. Individual greatness on its own does not mark you for immortality in St. Louis. It's only championships that do that.

Few people understand that truth better than Bob Forsch, who was drafted by St. Louis in June of 1968 and wore the "birds on the bat" on his chest for 15 seasons. When the Cardinals selected Forsch in the 26th round out of Sacramento, California, they were the reigning World Series champions, eight months removed from ending the "Impossible Dream" season of the Red Sox in the Fall Classic. By the end of the year, they'd won a third pennant in five seasons.

They were the dominant team in the National League, and arguably in all of baseball. It had been four years since the last Yankees pennant, while the Redbirds were making October their domain. St. Louis was in the midst of one of the great eras in the history of the franchise.

By the time Forsch reached the major leagues in 1974, many of the same names from that era were still around. Forsch's first Cardinals team included dynasty holdovers Brock, Gibson, and Tim McCarver, guys who had rings and could tell the kid first-hand about the glory years. Championships were fresh in the organization's memory, and more were expected. The veterans made it clear that there was a way you play Cardinals baseball. You played the game right, and you played to win.

"You'd always heard about Cardinal Baseball," Forsch said. "I learned from [instructor] George Kissell when I was in the minor leagues. There's Cardinal baseball, and there's a tradition behind it and a certain way to play it."

Things were starting to change in the won-lost column, though. Forsch's rookie season of 1974 marked the Redbirds' third runner-up finish in four years, so the club was still contending. But it was also the sixth straight season without a trip to the postseason. And the situation got worse, not better. That second-place finish was unequaled for the next seven seasons, as the St. Louis organization stumbled through the 1970s.

Gibson struggled through his last season and retired following the '75 campaign, hanging it up with 251 wins in 17 seasons—all as a Cardinal. That was the same year that Forsch established himself at the front of the rotation. Forsch's third season, 1976, found the Cardinals with a 72-90 mark—the franchise's worst record in 21 years—and a fifth-place finish, 29 games behind the first-place Phillies.

"I don't know what it was like in the '60s," Forsch said. "Wasn't there, don't know. But I know what it was like in the '70s. Baseball sort of looked forward to the beginning of the football season because

---

Bob Forsch was one of the few connections between two great Cardinals eras, the Gibson-Brock powerhouses of the 1960s and the "Whiteyball" teams of the 1980s. *Brace Photos*

it kicked us off the front page of the sports section so we didn't have to take the abuse."

The '77 team got an influx of youth and won 83 games, and Forsch won 20 for the only time in his career, but a year later the club backslid drastically. Forsch threw a no-hitter in 1978, but he did it for a team that lost 93 games. Brock retired after the '79 season, ending the last playing link to the 1960s powerhouses. In the four-season span between 1977 and 1980, five different men managed St. Louis. This was not what players or fans expect from one of baseball's most glorious and decorated franchises.

At the turn of the 1980s, though, things started to turn around. Whitey Herzog, who had managed three division winners in Kansas City, was hired to helm the club in 1980. A core of young talent started to establish itself, with names like Ken Oberkfell, Tom Herr, and Keith Hernandez coming into their own. Forsch was an old salt by that time, but he had yet to experience Cardinal glory.

"I was just trying to stay with the team when I first came up," Forsch said. "That was my opportunity to do well. And then in '75 they started turning the team over. I didn't understand what it took to have a championship team. I was on a really good team when I got there, but I was on a really good team because there were Gibsons, there were McCarvers. There were [Joe] Torres. There were Reggie Smiths. There were people like that. And then you're talking about a whole bunch of new guys who are coming in, who don't have those kind of credentials.

"And yet every time you go to Spring Training, you think you can win. Until you're in a situation where you do win, then you understand how all the components of talent have to come together. Having fun in the clubhouse, joking around before the game, relaxing that way. Everybody, regardless of whether they get along, they go out and play hard every day and never take a day off. That's what you start to understand. And that's what makes a winning ballclub."

Going into '81, Cardinals management made the first of two critical moves that would help complete the transition to a championship-caliber club. The December 1980 trade for Bruce Sutter gave St. Louis an elite relief pitcher to go at the back of the bullpen, helping to shore up what had been something of a weak point. And with Sutter in tow, the 1981 team deserved, by all rights, to play in the postseason. The '81 Cardinals went 59-43 for the best overall winning percentage in the National League East. But due to the midseason players strike, the season was divided into halves—and the Cardinals didn't win the first half or the second half.

"We had the best record [in '81] but we didn't get to go anywhere except home," Forsch recalls. "But it gave us the idea that hey, we had a pretty good team."

A year and a day after the Sutter trade, the Cards completed their second pivotal swap of the early '80s. Ozzie Smith was brought in from San Diego, making it two eventual Hall of Famers added to the roster in 366 days. The '82 Cardinals were ready for their close-up. As for Forsch himself, he was already 32—far from washed up, but it was unclear how many more chances he would have. He was a veteran on a mostly young team, but had no more playoff experience than any of his teammates. His best chance at October was dawning.

He and his teammates took advantage of that chance, starting on Opening Day. Forsch and the Redbirds beat Nolan Ryan and Houston at the Astrodome in their opener. By April 15, they were in first place. From there, they led the East for most of the remainder of the season. A brief bump in August dropped them to second, but from August 12 to the end of the season they spent just two days out of first place.

Joaquin Andujar and Forsch each won 15 games. Sutter topped 100 innings pitching out of the bullpen, and saved 36 games. Hernandez and George Hendrick had big years and a rookie named Willie McGee hit .296. Finally, the Cardinals were back in the postseason, winning the East by three games. The kiddie corps had meshed with a select group of elders, with Forsch in between.

"We had Jim Kaat, who played in the big leagues for a long time," Forsch remembers. "Gene Tenace was also there, and he had some outstanding playoff games with Oakland. So those two guys, one from a pitching standpoint and one from a player standpoint, knew what it was like to win. And I think we all fed off it.

"If somebody did something stupid over the course of the season in a game, Whitey didn't have to come and tell you, or have the coaches come and tell you. They would joke about it. And you knew—you knew they were talking about you. Or they'd just come right up to you and tell you. But it was never personal. It was always done in a joking way, but it was a learning experience at the same time."

That attitude, combined with the developing talent on the field, added up to a winner. The Cardinals hosted the surprising Braves in the National League Championship Series, both young teams three wins away from the World Series. Though most of them had never played in the postseason, the Cardinals knew right away what was in front of them. Their city made sure of it.

"You know how big the stakes are," Forsch said. "You've never been through it before, but when you get to the ballpark, St. Louis is the best. People come to the game all the time and have a good time, but there's just a different feel, a different atmosphere when it's play-off time.

"Walking through the parking lot, there's just a different spring in everybody's step going to the ballpark. I can't explain it. And it's not that people don't show up for all the games. But it's just a different—there's coolness in the air, it's just something."

There was something else in the air too, unfortunately: Game 1, a scheduled meeting of Andujar and knuckleballer Phil Niekro, was rained out in the fifth inning, just before it would have been an official game. Atlanta held the lead in the game, and Niekro was baffling the Cardinals. Yet the weather washed out the game. Officially, it was as though the first playing of Game 1 had never existed, and suddenly Forsch had opener duty again, just as he had back in April.

And just like in April, he was ready. And he dealt. Claudell Washington grounded out, opening the game. Rafael Ramirez grounded out. Dale Murphy, later named the National League's Most Valuable Player for '82, grounded out to end the inning. Three up, three down, no problem. Forsch hit his stride quickly.

"You never know when you're going to the ballpark, or when you're warming up in the bullpen," Forsch said. "I'd been pitching since '74 in the big leagues, and to me, throwing in the bullpen was sort of like hitting practice balls in golf. Sometimes you feel better, but there's not really that much of a correlation. I never put much stock in that.

"You never know how you're going to do until you go out between the lines. And it was amazing because somehow I got in a zone where you could pretty much put your mind in neutral. You saw everything. Where Porter put the glove, the ball went there."

In the second, Chris Chambliss and Bob Horner grounded out, and Jerry Royster struck out. Royster, a hometown friend of Forsch's, had always been a thorn in the righty's side. But on this day, he was no trouble.

"I guess [Royster] sort of knew that I was pitching him away, and he did hit a ball to right field, but George Hendrick was sitting there waiting for it," Forsch said. "Stuff like that, you think about years later, but it's just incredible how things worked out."

It remained scoreless into the third, as Braves starter Pascual Perez was looking strong too. After Glenn Hubbard struck out, an error by Oberkfell put No. 8 hitter Bruce Benedict on base in the third. Perez couldn't bunt him over, though, and it was an important miss. Washington singled, a hit that might have scored Benedict if Perez had gotten the bunt down. With two men on and two outs, Rafael Ramirez grounded into a force play to end the inning. Forsch was still in command. It was the closest thing to a jam he would see.

"When you get through a tough time early in the game, when you know you have good stuff and you get out of a situation like that, then it's like, 'Wow, I really do have good enough stuff to get out of any situation,'" Forsch said.

"You don't really even have to think about it from that point on. I didn't have to think too hard about throwing the ball on the outside corner; I'd just sort of throw it and it would go there. As opposed to thinking, 'Well I've got to start this ball six inches over the plate so that it runs.' I never had to think about anything like that."

In the fourth, he got a run to work with. It was a classic 1980s Cardinals run, resulting from speed and execution. McGee tripled, and Smith's sacrifice fly brought him home. It would be the only run Forsch would need, and he immediately got to the task of making it stand up.

"The biggest thing from a pitching standpoint, with a run early, if your team scores . . . the most important inning you have is when you go out there the next inning and shut them down," Forsch said. "Not let them score. Not walk the first guy that comes up to the plate."

No sweat. The heart of the Atlanta order accomplished nothing, with Murphy flying out foul and Chambliss and Horner both lining out. Royster, the pest, led off the fifth, and again Forsch sent him down, this time striking him out looking. Hubbard flied out and Benedict got on base again, this time with a single, but Perez hit a comebacker that ended the inning. With a single run still the margin, the speedy Washington led off the sixth with a single. But Porter gunned him down trying to steal second, and a threat was erased. A grounder and a popup gave Forsch his 17th and 18th outs. Six shutout innings were in the books.

Pitchers like Bob Forsch rarely, if ever, dominate. It's not how he operated. But Forsch knew he was in command this time.

"You're in a completely different zone," he said. "Nothing is hard. You don't have to think about throwing the ball just on the edge. It just goes there by itself. It just does. Bob Horner had a bad hand, so obviously we had to throw him in. And it was like every pitch was right in on his hands where it was supposed to be."

Then things got a lot easier. St. Louis racked up five runs against three pitchers in the bottom of the sixth, and suddenly Forsch had a cushion. Forsch himself even drove in a run in the rally, hitting a sacrifice fly. Everything was adding up, and the end was in sight for Forsch.

"The more runs you get, the better you feel," he said. "The good thing about pitching in October, it's cooler in the evenings. You're fresher longer. After you've thrown 200-plus innings already, your arm does start getting tired later on in the game, but that was one of those games where I didn't have to throw a lot of pitches. And I didn't feel like I threw a lot of pitches, even though I had a lot of strikeouts."

While his arm stayed strong, so did his concentration. Some pitchers say it's more difficult to pitch in a 6-0 game than a 1-0 game, but Forsch was just delighted to have the runs. He set down Chambliss, Horner, and Royster in order in the seventh, and the Cardinals were six outs from victory. Remarkably, Forsch was still picking up steam. Rather than letting down, he got stronger in the final third of the game, even after 233 regular-season innings. Glenn Hubbard flied out, Benedict struck out, and pinch hitter Larry Whisenton struck out looking. Forsch, never a strikeout pitcher, had made it his game. And there was no way he was leaving before it was over.

"[Herzog] may have talked it over with [pitching coach] Hub Kittle, I don't know," Forsch recalled. "But I was never in on it. That was the first playoff game I had ever pitched. So naturally you want to finish what you start. All these other years you've been watching playoff games on TV and thinking, 'Wow, I'd like to have the opportunity to do that sometime.' And then to have the opportunity to fulfill a dream, to have it come true, everybody wants to finish the game."

He did, and he did so in style. With the top of the order coming to the plate in a 7-0 game in the ninth, Forsch got three groundball outs, and the game was over. The Cardinals were one-seventh of the way to their first World Series title in 15 years. Forsch had given them just the kind of game you expect from a No. 1 playoff starter. Even if he wasn't supposed to be the No. 1 playoff starter.

It was the best game Forsch ever pitched, and that's saying a lot for a man who tossed two no-hitters. It's not just because of the circumstances, either. Forsch maintains that even in his no-nos, he didn't have everything at his disposal the way he did on October 7, 1982.

"I never felt like I was in any trouble," he said. "And if I was in trouble, I knew I had good enough stuff to get out of it. I don't know. You're just standing there and all of a sudden it's like you're king of the hill. You can get through anything."

Forsch was unable to recapture that feeling again in the '82 postseason, but it didn't matter. Despite two losses by Forsch in the World Series—one a rough game and one a respectable showing—the Cardinals took the big prize. Sutter recorded the final out in Game 7 against the Brewers, and the '82 Cardinals were the newest members of "the club."

Later down the road, Forsch summoned his playoff gem repeatedly. It stood as the gold standard for his starts, the closest Forsch could come to perfection on the mound. He had a VHS tape of the performances, one he would dust off when he needed to take a look at himself at his best. At first, he didn't have any way of watching the tape. But when you have something that valuable, you do what it takes.

"I went out and bought a VCR," he said. "I had the tape that was the entire tape of the game. I had it at home so I could look at it. And then they started having a video machine there at the ballpark. They had a camera behind home plate and down the line shooting across at you. So I could take my tape of a good game and put it on and see what I was doing, and put the tape where I pitched bad, and look at both of them. So when I'd throw between starts, I'd have something to work on.

"Did I use it every time I had a bad game? No, because when you're pitching, you're going to have peaks and valleys. You'll be really good for three games and bad for two. Every time you have a bad game, you can't say, 'Well, I have to go back and really see what I was doing wrong,' because that'll screw you up quicker than bad mechanics."

But when things got really rough, he always had that one game. Decades after his finest game, it's as though Forsch was that good every time he took the mound. If he's not a Cardinals icon like his old teammate Gibson, he's certainly a fan favorite and fondly remembered. He was a bright spot on bad teams in the '70s, and that would be worth plenty—much like Don Mattingly's place in the hearts of Yankees fans. But as a contributor to that '82 title, he means so much to so many fans, reaching another level in the Redbirds pantheon.

Forsch still enjoys going back to St. Louis, especially for playoff games. He revels in the atmosphere now, just as he did in October of 1982. And he pulls for his old team just like the fans who still remember him so vividly.

"When I go back now, people think I was a lot better than I was when I was actually playing," Forsch related. "They remember all the good times. They remember the World Series and playoff games and things like that. So you are held in high esteem.

"I won my 160 games or whatever, which is not a Hall of Fame career. But what happens is, I was fortunate enough to be in a situation. We went through really good years where it was very good times for the fans. They remember going to baseball games with their dads and now the tradition is carried on. They're taking their children to the game. And I think that's the great part about it. If there's a legacy about it, the legacy is in winning and Cardinal tradition."

Though he had to wait years and years, Forsch finally staked his claim to a piece of that legacy.

"I've got two pennant rings too, but the one I wear is my World

Series ring," he said. "You can go to the dance, you can be a bridesmaid, but it's not as good unless you're king or queen of the dance, or the bride or groom."

CHAPTER 5

JIM EDMONDS

Perceptions of Jim Edmonds changed drastically from when the outfielder was traded from the Angels to the Cardinals in the spring of 2000 to when he was shipped back to Southern California nearly eight years later. When the first deal came down, everyone knew St. Louis had acquired an elite talent, but the questions were numerous. Would Edmonds stay healthy and play enough to be an impact player? Was he a problem in the clubhouse? Did he care about anything other than looking good on the field?

Whatever the perception may have been, over his lengthy tenure wearing the "Birds on the Bat," Edmonds created a new image. He emerged as a team leader, a gamer, and a player who thrives when the game—or the season—is on the line. When Edmonds was sent away before the 2008 season, possibly to finish his career as a Padre, fans gave him a hero's farewell. Even those who understood the parting hated to see a franchise icon go somewhere else.

It was never clearer how Edmonds developed than when he was asked about his most memorable moment in a Cardinals uniform. The natural guess is his walk-off home run in Game 6 of the 2004 National League Championship Series, but the natural guess is wrong. Edmonds fast-forwards one night, to someone else's glory rather than his own. Not that he didn't play a part, but he was more the hors d'oeuvre for the night's baseball feast rather than the main course. His spectacular second-inning catch was pivotal, but Edmonds relishes the game for other reasons.

"Game 7 was special to me," he says. "My memories are of other people—Scotty [Rolen]'s home run in Game 7. I got to watch that. I always expect to do good things, so sometimes when you're in the moment, it doesn't really affect you. The two strikeouts in the playoffs and the World Series that [Adam] Wainwright had, stuff like that, I have a million of those. But I don't have a favorite moment of my own. I just think because I've been in awe my whole career of being able to do what I'm doing. It's kind of a weird thing for me."

This is the Edmonds who has received so much credit for St. Louis' 2006 run to the World Series title. It was Edmonds who began the custom of awarding a "game ball" to players who made big contributions in '06 playoff games. Edmonds enjoys being able to show off for the fans, but what he loves most about the game is his teammates. He knows it's a short list of people who truly understand the daily life in the major leagues. And he cherishes his relationships with the rest of the men in that tiny fraternity. When he can watch—or better yet, assist—in a teammate's moment of glory, that's as good as it gets.

"If you were asking me what my favorite game was, I would have to say Game 7 in '04," Edmonds says. "I made that play when the game was on the line, and I was on deck for Scotty's home run. It just was an exciting thing. The fans were really into it. Those are the things that I really remember. The walk-off homer was great. It looks great on TV, but it was just a spur of the moment thing, and I think it's more exciting to listen to the fans roar when somebody comes through than one single pitch for a home run. Everybody was on their feet when Scott was hitting."

The Cardinals didn't close the deal in '04, getting steamrolled by the Red Sox in the World Series after beating Houston, but simply winning a pennant felt like the top of the world in St. Louis, where it had been 17 years since the last National League championship. Ruling the Senior Circuit is considered a birthright of baseball by the Mississippi. So when that peak was scaled again, it was cause for raucous celebration. Even if they had to wait two more years before win-

---

Nobody brought drama and excitement to St. Louis baseball like Jim Edmonds, who livened up games with both his bat and his glove. *AP/WWP*

ning "The Ring," as manager Tony La Russa calls it.

"You can't really express the feelings," Edmonds says. "That's why it's hard to talk about. You can't express the feelings of what it's like to be in that position, or to go through that. I can't even imagine being Wainwright. That would be second to none."

Stardom was a long time coming for Edmonds, just as elder-statesman status was. He didn't hit his first professional home run until his second year in the minor leagues. He didn't reach double figures in long balls in a pro season until his fifth campaign, when he knocked the still less-than-overwhelming total of 14 between Double-A and Triple-A. Even in his first big league season, Edmonds hit all of five dingers in 94 games. "Hollywood" Edmonds, the man who later became known as much for big hits as anything else, didn't break out as a hitter until 1994—his seventh professional season, when he went deep 33 times as a California Angel.

Edmonds made his name first and foremost with the glove, and he has continued to make highlight reels for the remainder of his career. Despite offensive numbers that help make him a borderline Hall of Fame candidate, when most fans think of Edmonds, they think of spectacular catches and eight Gold Gloves. And so it fits that in the most memorable game he ever played, Edmonds made his mark not with his bat, but by flashing the leather in center field. His vital second-inning catch set the tone for a superbly played Game 7 of the National League Championship Series.

Later in the game, Edmonds' teammates swung the bats to beat Roger Clemens and the Astros. But in the second, Edmonds made the play of the night—the play that made it possible for his teammates' batting feats to matter. He chased down Brad Ausmus' deep line drive, saving at least two runs and preventing a big inning.

"I remember specifically in that playoff game being so excited that I was running faster than I thought I could run," he says. "I was really getting after it. Usually when you break on a ball, you just try to get yourself to top speed as fast as you can and then go true to the ball. There, I feel like I was digging a little bit harder."

"It was a spectacular play, but nothing out of the ordinary for Jimmy Edmonds," Ausmus told reporters later that night. "That may have saved the game for them." When you save the game with a catch in the second inning, you know you made a magnificent play.

Just one night before, Edmonds turned loose what surely was the most memorable moment in old Busch Stadium for many a fan. He throttled a Dan Miceli pitch in the 12th inning of Game 6 of the 2004 NLCS, forcing a Game 7 in one of the great series in recent baseball history. The '04 NLCS was dwarfed in television exposure by the Red Sox's comeback against the Yankees, but for quality of play, it was at least the equal of its more heralded American League counterpart. The 105-win Cardinals took the first two games in St. Louis, then dropped three in a row in Houston.

Every game had at least one lead change, and two of the games were decided by walk-off home runs. The drama and intensity were incessant, the home crowds frenetic. When the heavily favored Cardinals fell behind in the series, it looked like their spectacular season might end in another pennant-less year for the historic franchise.

But Edmonds would not let it be so. The Cardinals lost a 4-3 lead in the ninth inning, but the tie was preserved and the two rivals headed to extra innings. The 10th and 11th came and went without incident, as did the top of the 12th. In the bottom of the 12th, though, Albert Pujols drew a leadoff walk. Scott Rolen popped up, bringing up Edmonds, already established as a merciless Astro-killer. And he broke the hearts of Houston fans everywhere, drilling a mammoth homer and sending a crowd of 52,144 into delirium.

That home run was voted by Cardinals fans as the No. 6 most memorable moment in the 40 years of the second Busch Stadium (the one that stood from 1966-2005). It was the defining swing of one of the great seasons in the history of the St. Louis franchise and capped a spectacular baseball game. Yet Edmonds barely remembers it. He swung the bat, raised his arms in celebration, circled the bases, and was greeted at home by a frenzied flock of Cardinals. And then it was all over. In Edmonds' eyes, it was his teammates and the fans who truly got to enjoy his moment in the spotlight.

They took in the atmosphere while he prepared to hit against Miceli. They watched the flight of the ball, the majestic arc, and the distant landing. Edmonds was about the only person in the park who was not a spectator for his definitive dinger. He's seen it on video, but that's not the same.

"Obviously I'm a big fan of it, because it happened to me," Edmonds said. "But it's like everything goes blank when you're in the moment. I can hear the fans when I'm on deck, but I couldn't hear the fans when I was running around the bases. And they have a big role in how exciting things are. Those kinds of things that you see from a distance are almost more exciting than the things you have in your own feelings."

The next night, though, Edmonds got to enjoy his own moment. Then he got to revel in his teammates' time as well. He made one of the most stunning catches in franchise history, and maybe the best of his magnificent career. With the Redbirds trailing, he tracked down Ausmus' liner to keep a small deficit from becoming a big one. If it was Edmonds' greatest catch, that's no small statement, considering his heroics over the years—from Kansas City in 1997 to a string of at-the-wall home run thefts in St. Louis. But never did the degree of difficulty, the stakes, and the grace of the play all combine like they did in Game 7 against Houston.

"That's something you can't explain," Edmonds said after the game. "You'll have to ask somebody else. I haven't seen it. I don't know what it looked like."

A baseball game can be won or lost with a single swing, as Game 6 was by Edmonds the night before. It can be won or lost with a single pitch, such as when Adam Wainwright froze Carlos Beltran to end Game 7 of the 2006 NLCS. And, in a case like this one, it can be won or lost with something even simpler, more elemental—a single step.

Edmonds didn't take the time to process the stakes when he bolted after Ausmus' line drive. He didn't think about the possibility of a big inning, the potential that his team might lose its World Series dream before it got its second turn at bat. He didn't have the time to think about those things, even if he'd wanted to. He didn't really have the time to think about anything. He read and reacted. The message his brain delivered to his legs was simple, brief and entirely urgent: Go. Get to it. Now.

St. Louis already trailed by a run, and with Hall of Famer Clemens twirling for Houston, any larger deficit than that might have been hopeless. The Astros had two men on with one out against Jeff Suppan, a big-game pitcher but not a dominant one even on his best night. Ausmus stepped to the plate with a chance to do damage. And though the three-time Gold Glover and Dartmouth product has never been considered a threat offensively, he got the bat squarely on a Suppan pitch.

The ball took off, sizzling toward center field. Edmonds, who never played especially deep, was in even shallower than usual—a dangerous combination. So he didn't stop to think. He didn't worry much about an angle. He turned into a predator, and Ausmus' liner was his prey. Instinct ruled Edmonds.

"When he hit the ball, it was like, 'Uh oh, I *have* to catch this,'" Edmonds said. "In the playoffs, any mistake is probably going to break you. So all I can remember is just digging as hard as I could and saying, 'I *have* to catch this ball, no matter what.'"

This was not the "Hollywood" Edmonds that fans often think of. Edmonds, one of the truly spectacular defenders in baseball history, has sometimes been regarded with ambivalence, or worse. Because while his skills have always been undeniably tremendous, sometimes he was charged with making his catches look more impressive than they actually were. He always got to the ball, but sometimes the nagging suspicion existed that the catch didn't need to look quite so dramatic.

That wasn't the case in Game 7. This was Edmonds the ferocious competitor, the exemplary teammate, the man willing to do anything and everything to keep his team from falling behind even further. Repeatedly in past seasons, he thought he might finally taste the World Series, but the chance never came. He could remember his first season in a Cardinals uniform, 2000. The Redbirds swept the Braves in the Division Series, only to fall in five games to the Mets in the NLCS. Then there was the crushing 2002 disappointment, when a team that believed it was destined for glory fell short against the Giants in the NLCS.

He would not let this one slip away too. This team was too good, this season too special. They had worked too hard, for too long, to let a single mistake sink them. So he dug in. He kicked in the spurs on his horse and bolted full speed, without a single wasted movement, after Ausmus' liner. And he got there.

"When you play defense, and you're locked in that well, if you get a great jump, you think you can catch everything," he said. "I saw it the whole way, and I told myself, 'I have to catch it.' I do remember running harder, and thinking to myself, 'I'm running as hard as I possibly can right now.' Normally you try to glide to the ball so that the ball doesn't bounce. Because when the ball bounces in the outfield, it's impossible to catch."

It didn't bounce. That wasn't one of the acceptable options. Edmonds reeled it in. The runners didn't even advance, and the next batter, Clemens, struck out. A potential "crooked number" inning was kept to one, the visitors thwarted by Edmonds. A big-game player made his biggest play in one of the biggest games.

"The thought process is as quick as one step—everything has gone through my head," he explains. "I don't have time to think, 'Oh man, he made a bad pitch,' or, 'Oh, he hit it there.' Your body says, 'Dammit, I've got to go get this.' All in the same thought process. And as soon as you're moving, all that you're thinking about is catching it. I do remember sometimes telling myself, 'Dig, dig,' but there's no other thought process. Just go and catch it."

Craig Biggio had opened the game with a home run, the first time in baseball history that a Game 7 began with a homer—still more history in a series filled with media-guide moments. The series had already become the first LCS in history to have consecutive games end with walk-off home runs. It also set a record for the most long balls in an NLCS. It was that kind of series. But after Biggio's historic shot, Suppan retired Carlos Beltran, Jeff Bagwell, and Lance Berkman in order, keeping the deficit at a single run. The Cardinals, who had been quieted by Clemens over seven innings in Game 3, went 1-2-3 in the bottom of the first.

Clemens, in fact, had owned the Cardinals for quite a while. He posted a 2.36 ERA against them in the regular season. He mowed them down a year earlier at Yankee Stadium, picking up his 300th win and 4,000th strikeout in the same game. Every run the Astros could give Clemens got them that much closer to the franchise's first World Series.

So how did the second inning begin? With a free baserunner, of course. Jeff Kent walked to lead off the frame. Morgan Ensberg flied out with Kent on first base, but Jose Vizcaino singled to put men on first and second. Ausmus, known as a classic catch-and-throw catcher but no danger with the stick, came to the plate with Clemens on deck. And he connected.

"It wasn't a bad pitch," Edmonds said. "It was just like, I didn't have a choice to misread it or anything. It had to be caught. By the time I took a step, I was already saying, 'Run as hard as you can, and make sure you catch it.'"

Edmonds did. And a frenzied St. Louis crowd absolutely lost its mind. Edmonds may be known as a showman, but he insists he didn't even take one instant to enjoy the moment once the catch was made.

"That's when everything disappears," Edmonds said. "That's when I'm just doing my job. That's when it becomes my job. I think more about it going and getting it. Once I catch it, I say, 'OK, I've done my job, now get the ball back in.' I didn't hear anything. You lose all awareness of what's going on. Then you throw the ball back in and just go back to your position."

With the second out secured, Suppan went after Clemens and retired him to end the inning. Houston stretched its lead to two runs in the third, but it was the last tally the 'Stros would pick up. St. Louis got a run back in the bottom half of that inning, and in the sixth, Pujols and Rolen keyed a three-run outburst against Clemens that ultimately delivered the pennant. Had Edmonds not reeled in Ausmus' ball, though, the second might have broken the game open.

"I've played defense, and I guess you would say I've made some pretty good plays," Edmonds said. "But there's not a lot of those plays where I think, 'Oh, damn, I have to catch this ball.' It's usually just that you run the best route you can and get to the ball. There's only been a couple times when I've said, 'I've got to get this ball.'"

And of course, he did. Though he was certainly a part of the rest of the game, he'd put in his main piece. He got to spend a little time enjoying the other guys' curtain calls.

CHAPTER 6

BRUCE SUTTER

The Cardinals and the Cubs have made plenty of trades over the years that didn't amount to much. St. Louis' acquisition of Jeff Fassero in 2002, for example, didn't exactly grab the headlines or change the course of baseball history. But it does seem that when the two old rivals make a big splash of a deal, the Redbirds come out on top.

It happened in 1964, when St. Louis acquired Lou Brock for pitcher Ernie Broglio. Brock went on to a Hall of Fame career and was a key player on three pennant-winning teams. Broglio, a 21-game winner one year in St. Louis, won a grand total of seven games after the trade.

And then there's the Bruce Sutter trade, an economically motivated deal that wasn't nearly so one-sided, but still smells rosy from the St. Louis side of things. The Cubs acquired Leon Durham in the deal, a central part of their lineup for years afterward, so it wasn't a complete whitewash. But Sutter cemented his legend, won a ring, and earned his way into the Hall of Fame during his tenure in St. Louis. And the Cubs still haven't called to tell him he was dealt.

"I knew something was going to happen," Sutter says. "In '79, I won the Cy Young with the Cubs and we agreed, my agents and I agreed with Bob Kennedy, who was the general manager, on a five-year contract. But he had to have [owner William] Wrigley OK it. So we went down to Mr. Wrigley's office, and Mr. Wrigley pulled the contract offer off the table.

"We went to arbitration, and I was the landmark case in arbitration, where the Cubs went in at $350,000 and I went in at $700,000. And I won the case. My salary was almost triple anybody else on the Cubs. So I knew after that '80 season that there was a good chance I was going to get traded."

Following the 1980 season, Sutter was dealt to the team just a few hours down I-55.

"The thing about it is, it's funny—now I'm 54 years old and the Cubs still haven't called me and told me I was traded," he says.

"A reporter called. They never called me."

In his first year in St. Louis, Sutter played on a team that should have made the playoffs. The Cardinals won the most games of any National League East team, but the season was divided into two halves due to the strike. St. Louis didn't win the first half or the second half, and was deprived of the postseason appearance.

In '82, though, there were no such worries. Sutter and the Cardinals won the East by three games over the Phillies, earning their way into the playoffs for the first time since 1968. A transition had taken place over a stretch of several years in St. Louis. Trades for players like Ozzie Smith and Sutter played a role, as did the development of a talented young core. But Sutter points to the skipper, not the players.

"I played for the Cubs for five years and we played the Cardinals [a lot]," he said. "And one of the single things that changed St. Louis baseball and got it back to when [Bob Gibson] and Red [Schoendienst] and Lou and all them were playing was Whitey Herzog, when he came in as the manager and the general manager. He got the players that he wanted and put it all together, and really put Cardinal baseball back to where it was.

"With Whitey, there's nothing short of winning. If you didn't win, you lost. It didn't matter if you had a good season. If you didn't win the World Series, you didn't win. To me, he was the single most driving force."

So there was no debating the goal when the Cardinals reported to

---

Few players know the feeling Bruce Sutter experienced in 1982 when he recorded the final out for a World Series championship. *AP/WWP*

camp in '82. The expectation was the big trophy at the end of the year. They emerged from a fairly tight division race, then steamrolled the Braves in three games in the National League Championship Series. All that was left was the World Series, and a matchup with "Harvey's Wallbangers," the Harvey Kuenn-managed Milwaukee Brewers.

Sutter's first World Series appearance was an excellent one. He pitched 2⅓ shutout innings for the win in Game 2 as the Redbirds evened the series after losing the opener. But he struggled in each of his next two games. He allowed a homer, a walk, and two runs in Game 3, though it scarcely mattered because the Redbirds were ahead by five at the time. In Game 5, though, he gave up two costly eighth-inning tallies, which let Milwaukee turn a small lead into a safer one.

Games like that cause baseball people to say that closers must have a short memory. Sutter had one.

"That wasn't my first year," he says. "That's when it's tough, when you're young. But it was my seventh year of being a closer in the big leagues. I knew it was my job. Now, if I [struggled] for two weeks in a row, Whitey might have had different feelings. But there's always going to be a game where you go out there and, it's not even necessarily that you pitched bad, but the results are bad.

"The hitters are good. They hit good pitches. You learn to understand that about the game. Some days they're going to get you. And it doesn't mean you were horrible or you have to change anything. It just means that's the way it went that day. You learn to understand the game. It's not so much forgetting. It's more an understanding of how the game is."

Understanding that, Sutter was far from hesitant to get back in there. He was hungry for it. The Cardinals had dropped the last two games in Milwaukee before coming back home, meaning they needed to win twice at Busch Stadium to win it all. Starter John Stuper and a relentless offensive attack provided a 13-1 blowout win in Game 6, ensuring there would at least be a Game 7.

Sutter wasn't needed in that game, meaning he'd had two days off thanks to the travel day between Games 5 and 6. He knew what that meant, and so did Herzog. The manager wouldn't hesitate to turn to his security blanket early. The three-out closer of modern times didn't exist yet in 1982.

"I remember thinking about that when I went home," Sutter says. "I didn't sleep much that night, because I knew that seventh game, Herzog told me he wasn't going to go to me before the sixth inning."

He laughs when he says this, realizing how much times have changed. It's unthinkable now that a manager would even consider using his No. 1 reliever before the eighth, never mind the sixth. And Sutter also realized that if he pitched, he'd be throwing the biggest pitches of his life—the biggest pitches in St. Louis in 14 years.

"I knew that there was going to be a heck of a chance that I was going to throw the pitch to win that, or to lose it," he says. "I didn't sleep well. All day I was jittery. And I usually didn't get like that. But for that game, it was something that affected me the whole day. I didn't want to eat. I was nervous. I was real jittery."

Sutter couldn't even stand sitting at home on October 20. It was just too much. He was paid to keep his cool, but that only applied while the game was going on. Nothing in his contract said he couldn't get tight in the afternoon.

"Gene Tenace and I went to the ballpark every day together, and I think we left at 12:30 or something for a seven o'clock game," Sutter says. "Just to get down there, get in the locker room, get around the guys, and maybe get it out of my system."

The Cardinals sent Joaquin Andujar to the mound for Game 7, and if Andujar's behavior could be erratic at times, no one doubted his toughness or desire. Andujar had been struck by a Ted Simmons base hit in Game 3, forcing him out of the game, and some outside the Cardinals clubhouse wondered whether he would pitch the finale. His teammates had no such worries. They wanted Andujar out there, and they were certain he would be.

"As players, we knew Joaquin was going to pitch," Sutter says. "But there was so much being made out of whether he was going to pitch or not, or how he was going to pitch, or if he was hurt, whatever. But we knew Joaquin. He was going to pitch that day and he was going to pitch well."

Andujar did not disappoint. He and Pete Vuckovich exchanged zeroes in the first three innings. In the middle frames, though, it became a back-and-forth game. Lonnie Smith's RBI single in the fourth put the homestanding Cardinals ahead, 1-0. Milwaukee tied it in the next half inning when Ben Oglivie hit a leadoff homer against Andujar, and the Brew Crew added two more in the sixth. Paul Molitor picked up an RBI single, and Cecil Cooper added a sacrifice fly for a 3-1 Brewers lead.

That lead didn't stand any longer than the Cards' had, though. In the bottom of the sixth, five straight Cardinals reached base. Keith Hernandez and George Hendrick each hit an RBI single for the fourth and fifth base runners, putting St. Louis back ahead by a 4-3 count. Sutter knew his time was about to come.

"At old Busch Stadium, the bullpen was just right down the right-field line, and I found it was better for me to stay in the dugout," Sutter recalls. "Whitey could just turn around. The people could hang over you there and talk to you in the dugout, and you couldn't really watch the game. And I liked to get into the flow of the game. So I'd stay in the dugout, and Whitey could just turn around and say, 'You're in.'"

At the start of the Milwaukee half of the seventh, Herzog alerted his closer to start getting ready. He definitely didn't need the phone, as Sutter was sitting directly behind him, practically breathing on his neck. Sutter made the short jog down to the bullpen as Gorman Thomas batted in the seventh, and the chant started. Busch Stadium's crowd of 52,723 began yelling "BRUUUUUCE" for their hero.

"I knew that once we got the lead or tied in the seventh game of the World Series, I was going to be the pitcher," Sutter says. "It was just a matter of when. And so starting in the fifth inning, I'm ready now. I'm ready to go. I've done all my stretching. I've done all my exercise. And all it took was just that look, and I knew it was on. That's when the switch really kicks in."

As long as Andujar was going well, though, there was no hurry to get to Sutter. And Andujar was going well. He struck out Thomas at the end of a tough seven-pitch at-bat. Roy Howell flied out, and Charlie Moore beat out an infield single. Sutter was ready but still wasn't really needed. It was actually an out—not a hit—that convinced Herzog that the time had come to go to the pen.

Jim Gantner hit a comebacker to Andujar, who handled it cleanly and tossed it to Hernandez at first. Gantner apparently felt Andujar showed him up on the play, though, and expressed his displeasure to the pitcher. Andujar didn't take that well, and the two began jawing at each other. Andujar had to be restrained by umpire Lee Weyer before pitching coach Hub Kittle was able to get out to help. At that moment, Herzog knew he had to lift his starter before Andujar sidetracked himself.

"As soon as Joaquin got mad," Sutter remembers, "he said, 'That's it. You're in.'"

Sutter entered the game with a tough assignment. He faced the first, second, and third hitters of a very dangerous offense, with a one-run lead and six outs still to go. Milwaukee's lineup featured six batters who hit at least 19 home runs that year, and the Brewers led the majors by a large margin in runs scored on the season.

In a seventh game, with a narrow lead, Sutter had no room for error. The Busch Stadium crowd greeted him with another "BRUU-UCE" cheer, and Sutter realized that he was in the situation for which he'd waited his entire life.

"You have Robin Yount and Paul Molitor in the Hall of Fame, and Teddy Simmons should be in the Hall of Fame," says Sutter, now a Cooperstown enshrine himself. "You had Cecil Cooper, who was a great player. You had Gorman Thomas, who was a home-run hitter. Ben Oglivie was a home-run hitter. Yount and Molitor both had over 3,000 hits. You get one guy on base and one of those guys crank one, the game goes the other way."

Sutter, however, came out with ferocious stuff. He started Molitor with a trademark split-finger fastball, a nasty, diving pitch that Molitor fouled off. Molitor chased another split to fall behind 0-2. Once you were behind Sutter that far in the count, you had no chance. His famous split started in the zone and dove out of any kind of hitting range, inducing feeble, foolish-looking swings at pitches that weren't even strikes.

After Sutter missed with the 1-2 pitch, he gave Molitor still another splitter. Molitor beat it into the dirt, grounding to shortstop. It was more of the same for Yount, who also fell behind 0-2 when he took a splitter and fouled off another one. He fouled away an 0-2 pitch before chasing a split-finger pitch in the dirt for strike three.

Again came the chants of Sutter's name, and Busch Stadium was shaking. Cooper swung at the first pitch from Sutter, grounding to second base, and the Cardinals were three outs from the big prize. Sutter made his way to the dugout to watch his teammates try to get him some runs.

"It's kind of like a double-edged sword," he explains. "You want to get more runs, because that makes your job a little bit easier. But by the same token, you're pitching well, you've got the other team down, let's finish it. So you want them to score runs, but you want them to do it quickly. Two outs, boom, base hit, two-run homer would have been fine."

They did get him two more runs, though they didn't do it very quickly. Darrell Porter and Steve Braun each hit a two-out RBI single, stretching the lead to 6-3.

"It was a matter of sitting there waiting for the inning to get over and get out there," Sutter said. "I remember telling [equipment manager] Buddy Bates, 'I'll be right back.'"

The second inning, though, was a little tougher. Sutter's split didn't have quite the same bite in the ninth, though it was still good. However, he had an advantage in the ninth that he didn't have in the eighth.

"I was going to pitch my game," he says, "especially in the ninth inning when I had the three-run lead. But back then, when a team was down two or three runs in the ninth inning, they would take the first strike. And Milwaukee was a team that did that, and we knew that going in.

"So then I would throw a first-pitch straight fastball to get strike one. Then I would go to the split-finger. Some teams did it, some teams didn't. But Milwaukee, they were a veteran team and they knew they couldn't hit a three-run homer with nobody on base. They took the first strike and I knew that, so that changed my philosophy a little bit."

The tactic made sense in the abstract, but was a little harder to justify against a pitcher like Sutter. Giving Sutter a strike was simply inviting him to take you further and further out of the zone with his splitter. True to form, Simmons took a fastball over the plate to start his at-bat. He took a splitter out of the zone to get even in the count, but hit a comebacker for the third-to-last out.

Oglivie likewise took a first-pitch strike, and then a fastball up and in for a 1-1 count. That set up a splitter that Oglivie swung at and missed to go to 1-2. Once again, ahead in the count, Sutter came with a split-finger down and probably out of the zone, and Oglivie swung at it. He grounded to second. Two down.

It's a common belief that the toughest out of a game is the 27th, though, and Sutter surely found that to be the case against Milwaukee. Thomas, like his predecessors, took a fastball for an 0-1 count. He took the next two pitches as well, but both were balls. Thomas swung and missed at a split-finger to even the count, and then the battle really heated up.

Thomas fouled off a pitch to stay alive, then took ball three on a pitch barely outside the zone. He drilled a line drive down the left-field line but fouled, then fouled off two more pitches. Nine pitches in, and the battle was still not decided. Catcher Darrell Porter put a sign down, and Sutter shook him off. He threw Thomas a fastball up and out over the plate, Thomas chased it, and the World Series was over.

Sutter raised one fist high in the air, Porter came out to hug him, and it was dogpile time.

"What a feeling that is," Sutter says. "It's something to go through a season with 25 guys. And the goal you set out for in the second week of February, your goal is to win the World Series. To finally do it, what a feeling that was.

That was my seventh year in the major leagues and my first time ever in the playoffs. The whole season was just magical, and those guys . . . what a great bunch of guys."

A large print of Sutter's celebration hung downstairs at old Busch Stadium until the park was torn down. A similar image now hangs in the pitcher's home.

"The baseball stuff was always in the back rooms with trunks and stuff," he says. "But I built a bar down in my basement, and [my sons] wanted me to put all the baseball stuff out. So I have a big picture of me with my fist up in the air after the last strikeout. I have the World Series jerseys. It's an important part of my life. My boys, they grew up baseball fans and they like looking at all the stuff."

Sutter pitched only two more years in St. Louis, making it a four-season tenure wearing the "Birds on the Bat." He pitched five years in Chicago before he was dealt to the Cardinals, and was on the Braves payroll for six years afterward—though due to injuries, he pitched in only three seasons for Atlanta.

Yet when he was inducted in Cooperstown, the Hall of Fame

chose a Cardinals hat for him. Thanks to that World Series, Sutter will always be most associated with his time as a Cardinal.

"I think it's because of the teams that we had there in St. Louis, and that's why the Hall of Fame saw fit to put me in as a Cardinal," he says. "My boys were a little bit older then when I was with St. Louis, and that's what they remember. So I think that most people associate me with the Cardinals. World Series champions, that's what people remember."

He won a Cy Young in Chicago. He made big money in Atlanta. But he won his ring in St. Louis. And the ring is the thing that sticks with you forever. He was only a Cardinals player for four years, but he'll be a Cardinal for the rest of his life.

"Ex-players are always welcome there. The way Tony [La Russa, current manager] welcomes us in the locker room, and the way the current players treat us when we come back, we're all one big family. I think that's part of the Cardinals' history and part of the mystique.

"We all know what it's like to play in St. Louis. We know what the fans expect. You're expected to win. And we all know what that feels like. It's a great feeling. And it's great to be appreciated."

CHAPTER 7

TOM
HERR

Tom Herr had already seen plenty in the major leagues, and as a Cardinal, by the time the 1985 season unfolded. Herr was there at the end of the 1970s and the dawn of the '80s, when the franchise was putting the pieces together for a rise out of irrelevance. He played on the 1981 team that got cheated out of a playoff spot, winning the most games in the National League East but not winning the first or second half.

He played a vital role as the keystone corner man on the '82 World Series champions, bringing the trophy back to St. Louis for the first time in 15 years. And he entered his offensive prime in 1983 just as the Cardinals took a step back, missing the playoffs in '83 and again in '84. Herr was only 29 when the '85 season started, but he was one of the veterans of an increasingly seasoned team. But he'd never seen the likes of what was to come in that memorable campaign.

It was as though everything was played under brighter lights, on a bigger stage, in '85. St. Louis, the National League's most historic franchise, locked horns all year long with the rising Mets—who were establishing themselves as media darlings as well as a good ballclub. The two teams combined for 199 wins and finished three games apart, sparking what would be the league's best rivalry in the second half of the decade.

And the postseason . . . oh, the postseason. The Cardinals battled the Dodgers in the first best-of-seven National League Championship

Series, a series that featured not one but two of the best-known home runs in Cardinal chronicles. Then they hooked up for the "I-70 Series" against the Royals, a World Series that turned on one of the most infamous calls in baseball history—Don Denkinger's safe call on Jorge Orta in Game 6.

"It certainly was a bigger stage for us," Herr says. "I think it was kind of the beginning of the evolution of media coverage of the play-offs, to the point where today it's such a spectacle that the game becomes kind of secondary to the television coverage. The concerns of the players and the comfort of the players has taken such a back seat to the networks that I think it's really gone too far the other way.

"But back in the middle to late '80s was kind of the start of the networks figuring out that, 'Hey, we can get some really good ratings and make a lot of money televising these playoffs the right way.' And I think expanding the series to a best of seven was really what started that."

If the early '80s were *Little House on the Prairie* in St. Louis and in baseball, then '85 was more like *Miami Vice*. The game was the same as always, but the trimmings were definitely changing. Fortunately for the Cardinals, when they got to the playoffs, they had already been well seasoned. Though they won 101 games, they surely did not run away with the National League East. As late as October 2, following a home loss to the Mets, they led New York by one game with four to play.

The Mets were already drawing notice not only for their ability but their personality. The swashbuckling team that would win it all in '86 was largely in place, with Gary "The Kid" Carter and Keith Hernandez at the core. Young talents like Darryl Strawberry, Lenny Dykstra, and of course Dwight Gooden were emerging, giving Cardinal fans targets for their ire for years to come.

Not that the Redbirds were anything to dismiss. Like in New York, an already good St. Louis team received an infusion of young talent, headed by sensational speedster Vince Coleman. They led the league in scoring, getting on base, stealing bases, and triples. They

Tom Herr did something almost unheard of in 1985, when he drove in 110 runs on just eight home runs. *AP/WWP*

allowed the second-fewest runs in the National League. They played superior defense and always played with élan.

"It was an incredible pennant race that year between us and the Mets," Herr remembers. "It was a very dynamic team. It was one of the most unusual teams I think in baseball history, in that there were five switch-hitters in the lineup who played every day—Vince Coleman, Willie McGee, myself, Ozzie Smith, and Terry Pendleton. That in itself is so rare, so odd that a team could have five switch-hitters in the lineup and be successful."

The Cardinals had the MVP, Willie McGee, and the Rookie of the Year, Coleman. The Mets had the Cy Young winner in Gooden. The Cards had five All-Stars, the Mets four.

Going to Los Angeles was no walkover, but the Cardinals knew they'd been tested plenty already. They were confident, if not overconfident. Then they went to Dodger Stadium. Upon arriving in Los Angeles, they ran into an overwhelming and somewhat intimidating environment. And more to the point, they ran into a pair of superb young starting pitchers. Gooden won the Cy Young that year, but the Dodgers had two of the top five finishers in the voting.

A very good, 95-win Dodgers team trotted out its two aces in Games 1 and 2, and they took it to the Redbirds. Fernando Valenzuela, who won 17 games with a 2.45 ERA in '85, pitched $6\frac{1}{3}$ solid innings before handing off to closer Tom Niedenfuer in the seventh in Game 1. The Dodgers won, 4-1.

A day later, the Dodgers turned to their "bulldog," Orel Hershiser, and the righty pitched a classic Hershiser game. He didn't dominate, but he won. Hershiser actually issued more walks (five) than he collected strikeouts (four), but he went the route in an 8-2 win. Joaquin Andujar, one of the Cards' own co-aces along with John Tudor, was lit up for six runs. The Cards were fortunate it wasn't a year earlier, or they would have been one game from elimination rather than two. Even so, they were in a tough situation as they headed home to St. Louis.

"It's certainly not a position you want to be in," Herr acknowledges. "It makes Game 3 a must-win situation. If you go down 0-3, the odds are so stacked against you that you almost lose hope at that point. But if you're going home and you get that Game 3 and get the momentum back on your side, get one in the win column—that changes everything. So our focus going back to St. Louis was just on Game 3. Let's get that win and see what happens."

And what do you know? Back at home, the Cardinals got their win. On a Saturday afternoon, they jumped out to a 4-0 lead and held on for a 4-2 win, getting back in the series.

The day of Game 4 got off to a terrible start when Coleman was injured in a run-in with the automatic tarp machine, but his team-mates rallied for him. They obliterated Jerry Reuss, as Tudor came back on short rest to pitch seven innings of one-run ball. The Cards steamrolled the Dodgers, 12-2, and just like that it was a three-game series.

For practical purposes, though, it felt a lot like a one-game series. If the Dodgers had won, they would stanch the bleeding. They'd be going back home with two chances to win a single game. If the Cardinals won, they'd be riding a huge wave, and they'd have Andujar back on the mound with a chance to finish it off. Los Angeles, which had held both its aces back, sent Valenzuela out for a second start, with Hershiser lurking in Game 6. St. Louis brought out Bob Forsch for his first start of the series. The pitching matchup, at least, favored the visiting Dodgers.

Yet the Redbirds jumped ahead of Valenzuela, taking a 2-0 lead in the first before the Dodgers tied it in the fourth. The score remained tied until the bottom of the ninth, with Valenzuela rolling while the Cards cycled through four pitchers. In the last of the ninth, though, Smith hit one of the peaks that defined his legend. Facing Niedenfuer, the Dodgers' big, hard-throwing relief ace, Smith socked the first left-handed home run of his career.

The Cards had the momentum. They had the series lead. And they had established that they could beat Niedenfuer.

"He was their guy," Herr remembers. "He was a very effective closer. He was a big, strong, hard-throwing guy with a heavy fastball. And he wasn't just a three-out closer. He was a guy who could come in and get you five or six outs if he needed to. He was tough. He gave us trouble throughout the year when we played them during the reg-ular season.

"It was so shocking because Ozzie certainly wasn't a guy who got the ball elevated a whole lot. His whole thing was to try to hit line drives and groundballs, whatever it took to get on base with his speed.

So to get a home run from him, especially a game-winning home run, was just electrifying."

On the Sunday night flight west, for the first time the Cardinals felt that they were in command. They had their swing back, and they were ready to finish things off and return to the World Series for the second time in four years.

"That's when we really felt we were going to win this thing," Herr says. "That was huge. Valenzuela pitched that game, too. I think once we went up 3-2, we felt like—this is ours to win."

Game 6 brought a rematch of the series' second game, but a much more competitive version. Andujar wasn't brilliant but neither did he get knocked around. And for six innings, Hershiser was Hershiser. The Cardinals trailed early, as Bill Madlock slapped an RBI single in the first inning and Mariano Duncan followed suit in the second. Herr singled home Andujar in the third, but in the fifth a sacrifice fly and a solo homer stretched the Los Angeles lead to 4-1.

Herr says the visiting dugout never felt downtrodden, even when the Redbirds were down to their last nine outs.

"I don't think you ever lose hope, unless it's just a blowout," he says. "We felt like we had not really been able to get anything going up to that point, and we just felt like all it was going to take was to have one inning where things went our way. We felt like if we could do that, we could pull it out late."

That one inning was the seventh. Darrell Porter and Tito Landrum each singled before Steve Braun grounded to first base for the first out. The runners advanced, giving MVP McGee a chance to drive in two runs. Conveniently, that's just what the '85 National League batting champion did. He laced a two-run single, making it 4-3 and chasing Hershiser.

That was the good news. The bad news was that Hershiser was replaced by Niedenfuer—hardly a break for the St. Louis hitters. Yet Smith greeted Niedenfuer with another extra-base hit, this time a triple that scored McGee and tied the game.

"For us to get three to tie it was huge," Herr says. "We felt like we were better at the end of the game than they were. We felt like our bullpen was better with [Todd] Worrell down there. We could match up left-hander/right-hander with guys like [Jeff] Lahti and [Ricky] Horton and Ken Dayley and so forth. We felt like we were better and deeper in the bullpen. So once we got tied, you're basically down to a two-inning game and we felt like we were better armed to get through that."

They had a chance to take the lead in the seventh, though, and missed it. Los Angeles intentionally walked the switch-hitting Herr in order to face the dangerous—but right-handed—Clark. And it worked. The slugger struck out, as did Andy Van Slyke, and the Dodgers escaped with the tie intact.

"Jack was intense," Herr says. "He was a fierce competitor. At that time, in the National League, if he wasn't the most feared slugger in the league, he was in the top three. And what made him so different from the other guys was that he swung the bat with such ferocity. He would take a rip at everything. He never got cheated.

"He was a guy that did strike out a lot, but that was part of his approach. That was part of his makeup. And you accepted that from him, because you knew that at some point he was going to get the guy. Believe me, you always wanted him up there in that situation."

Fortunately, he got another shot. Niedenfuer pitched a perfect eighth, but Worrell gave up a leadoff homer to Mike Marshall in the bottom of the inning. After all the fight to come back, one swing had put the Cardinals behind again.

They had three outs left to secure the win, or face a Game 7 at Dodger Stadium. And history has not been kind to teams that lose Game 6 on the road and have to come back for a seventh contest. Niedenfuer came out for a third inning, and Cesar Cedeno pinch hit for Worrell. He struck out, but McGee picked up another single. McGee stole second, and Smith walked.

The Cardinals actually made a move that looked like it might take the bat out of Clark's hands. Manager Whitey Herzog called on Herr to bunt the runners over, which would have brought up Clark with two outs and an empty base. Despite the lefty Van Slyke lurking after Clark, it seemed clear that Dodgers manager Tommy Lasorda would choose to face Van Slyke rather than Clark.

Herr didn't get the bunt down, but he got the runners over just the same. His grounder to first made it second and third with two outs, and Clark at the plate. And with that, he was a spectator just like everyone else at Chavez Ravine.

"I fouled a couple off, and with two strikes, [Herzog] let me swing away," Herr says. "And at that point you're just trying to put the ball in play. I was fortunate enough to pull the ball to the first baseman. And with the speed we had on base, they couldn't get a force at second. They had to take the out at first."

Herr, like his teammates, the press and fans all over, was doing the calculations in his head at that point. What would the Dodgers do? What should they do? He came to the same conclusion as most others—that Clark probably wouldn't get a chance to hit. But Lasorda had seen his pitcher fan Clark three innings earlier. He went with strength against strength.

"Niedenfuer was in his third inning of work," Herr says. "I believe they had Jerry Reuss ready in the bullpen, and we kind of thought they would walk Jack and go after Van Slyke with the left-hander. But Tommy decided to let Niedenfuer face Jack, and I think it all goes back to the previous at-bat when Niedenfuer struck him out."

Clark punished the Dodgers for their decision. He crushed a three-run homer to left field that put the Cardinals back in front, 7-5. Van Slyke popped up, and the Cardinals had pulled within three outs of the pennant.

"It was such an electrifying moment," Herr recalls. "Just his reaction after he hit it. It was one of those balls where you don't even have to watch it. The split-second it hits the bat, you know it's gone. It was extremely exciting.

"The only bad part about it was that we had to regroup and go out there and get some more outs to win the game. But at that point, it was such a huge blow that deflated the Dodgers. They really didn't have anything left to mount anything in the last inning."

Herzog summoned Ken Dayley, who went about his business quickly and efficiently. Dayley needed a mere nine pitches to finish off the game. He struck out Duncan and Enos Cabell, and Pedro Guerrero flied out.

The best team in the National League was going to represent the Senior Circuit in the World Series. And the pennant was back where the Cardinals believed it belonged—flying at Busch Stadium. Clark had come through, and so had his teammates.

"He was a guy that we liked to have up there in that situation," Herr says. "So it was neat that he got a chance to be up there again in the ninth inning. But believe me, he was also a guy that nine out of 10 times in that situation with an open base, teams were not going to face him. He was the guy in our lineup that you look at him and say, 'We're not going to let him beat us.' That was a key part of that whole scenario, that he even got a chance to swing the bat in that situation."

Two decades later, it's Smith's homer that's most famous in Cardinals lore, for a variety of reasons. It's identified with Jack Buck's iconic call—"Go crazy, folks! Go crazy!" It happened at home. And it came off the bat of Smith, one of the most loved Cardinals in history.

But for those who were there, Clark's hit was the biggest. Smith's may have been the bigger story, but it was Clark who killed off the Dodgers. It's the final game, not the better-known home game, that resonates with Herr.

"The Clark home run is always the first one that comes to my mind because of the stage that it occurred on," Herr says. "It was Game 6, a deciding game. It was against the Dodgers in L.A. There are a lot of factors that contributed to his home run being so huge.

"At the time, it was kind of like the Shot Heard Round the World in the St. Louis area. 'Where were you when Jack hit the home run?' was almost like, 'Where were you when Kennedy was shot?' It was such a historic thing in that region."

The sad fact for Herr and Cardinal Nation, though, is that both homers were dwarfed by an even more memorable play a few days later.

The Cards roared into the World Series on a high, facing the Royals and once again beginning on the road. They took leads of 2-0 and 3-1 in the series, but with a 3-2 series advantage and a 1-0 lead in Game 6, they couldn't close it out.

Denkinger made himself an enemy to Cardinals fans everywhere when he ruled Jorge Orta safe on a close play at first base, and that hit set up a winning rally for the Royals. Kansas City went on to win Game 7 and the series. The Cardinals were heartbroken and left with a slew of what-ifs. Not only the call caused second thoughts, but also the absence of Coleman. It's a loss that still sits poorly with players and fans.

But it's not enough to ruin the memories of a tremendous series. Herr remembers the World Series, but he cherishes the NLCS win more than he stews over the World Series loss. He saw a lot, but nothing quite like that day.

CHAPTER 8

ERNIE BROGLIO

Despite the fact that he's most famous for being traded away from St. Louis, Ernie Broglio still feels quite an affinity for the town where he first made his big-league name. More than four decades after his retirement, Broglio still attends Cardinals functions and is still warmly welcomed by fans. He lives in Arizona, and he finished his career with the hated Cubs. But like so many of his teammates and successors, he's still a Cardinal at heart. And he always will be.

"St. Louis is a great city," Broglio says. "I respected those baseball fans tremendously. When I was there, they were coming from Tennessee, they would travel hours and hours to come to a doubleheader. These people would travel hours and hours, and then go back to their job on a Monday. And I would just sit there and think about all these people, how they would travel. And that respect for the organization, I don't know if it had to do with Stan Musial or the Gas House Gang or what, but I just believe that the people brought out a lot of what we did on the field."

In the years since Broglio called it a career, his name has become synonymous with bad trades. Many fans who weren't even born when he played can rant about Brock for Broglio. What many of them don't know is that in 1964, it appeared that the Cardinals were taking a bigger risk than the Cubs were. Broglio was established, and he was in his prime. He was a 28-year-old pitcher with a 21-win season and an 18-win season to his name already. He'd tossed more than 220 innings three times, and more than 170 in each of his five seasons.

He was no scrub. The Cubs wanted Broglio to shore up their rotation, which coincidentally was headed up by another former Cardinal, Larry Jackson. They parted with an eventual Hall of Famer in Lou Brock, but it was Brock who looked like the long shot at the time. So it's somehow fitting that in a trade that worked out so well for the Redbirds, both of the principals now associate with St. Louis. Broglio came up in the Giants system, was dealt to the Cardinals and later to the Cubs, but he's a Cardinal in retirement.

"I had been in one other organization, and then I [later] went to another organization," he says. "And in my experience there was no organization like the Cardinals. They install that belief that you do good, try hard, and win. And I think with guys like Ken Boyer, Stan Musial, Curt Flood, and Bill White, we just had ballplayers on that team that made it comfortable to play the game."

Broglio bridged two eras of Cardinals baseball, like Terry Moore before him and Bob Forsch after him. When he came up in 1959, he joined a team with Musial—the greatest Cardinal of them all—and Boyer. When he was traded away, he left the burgeoning nucleus of the next great St. Louis dynasty, with Bob Gibson, Flood, and the man with whom he traded places, Brock. He never got to enjoy the highs of the Cards run in the late '60s. But unlike Brock, he did get to play with "Stan the Man," easily the most revered figure in the history of the franchise.

"He did nothing but sit there and talk with you, whatever you wanted to talk about," Broglio remembers. "He never shied away because he was a superstar and you were a peon."

And on August 11, 1960, with Musial pushing 40 years old and Broglio not yet 25, the superstar made the youngster a winner in the greatest game Broglio ever pitched. Musial's extra-inning home run delivered a lead for Broglio, and the pitcher made it stand up.

The 1960 season marked a return to relevance for a proud franchise after a long fallow run. The Cardinals were the National League's dominant franchise in the 1940s, but the '50s treated them unkindly. From 1954-59, St. Louis had five losing seasons out of six

Ernie Broglio is much more than the answer to a trivia question. Before he was traded for Lou Brock he was a 21-game winner in a Cardinals uniform.
Brace Photos

and only once finished in the first division. The '60 club, though, had a different cast to it. Julian Javier made his debut that year, while White, Flood, and Gibson were developing stars in their second season wearing the "Birds on the Bat." An 18-year-old kid named Tim McCarver barely played, but he was learning his way around the major league clubhouse. In December of '59 alone, the Redbirds made four separate trades as they began building the next great era.

And for the first time in a long time, the Cardinals were in a race. In mid-August, they headed east to Pittsburgh to play another newly ascendant team, the league-leading Pirates. The second-place Cards trailed the Buccos by five games at the start of the four-day, five-game series, giving them plenty of chance to gain ground in the standings. They had won in Philadelphia the day before, 6-5 in 10 innings, overcoming five errors and an early 3-0 deficit.

For the opener at Forbes Field, on August 11, they sent Broglio to the mound to face Bucs right-hander Bob Friend. Along with Vernon Law, Friend was one of the Pirates' top starters. Broglio, meanwhile, had been the Cards' lucky charm of late. They had won each of his previous four starts, and nine of his past 10. Broglio had also won his only previous start against Pittsburgh in '60. So the Cards started the series in Pittsburgh with plenty of good feeling, and plenty of incentive.

"You only had eight teams, and out of the eight teams, all the teams had good ballplayers," Broglio says. "So you just went into every series, whether it's the first part of the season, middle part of the season, or last part of the season, with the attitude that you're looking to October. I think that's what we were looking at. But it was the last part of the season, so it made it even better."

Broglio had one other advantage working for him. Pirates star Roberto Clemente, who emerged in '60 as one of the great players in the game, was unavailable. Clemente's place was taken by Gino Cimoli—a capable player, but no Hall of Famer.

Friend sent down the Cardinals in order in the first, and Bill Virdon opened the game for Pittsburgh with a single. But after Dick Groat struck out, Broglio essentially announced his m.o. for the rest of the evening. No. 3 hitter Bob Skinner hit into a 3-6-1 double play.

"If you're not walking anybody, and you're continually around the strike zone, you're going to get those double-play balls," Broglio says.

"You want to throw strikes. You don't want to walk people when you've got a defensive team like that."

Broglio was happy to take advantage of the defense behind him, and it was excellent. He had Gold Glovers at both corners in first baseman Bill White and third baseman Ken Boyer, and quality defenders up the middle, too, with shortstop Darryl Spencer and second baseman Julian Javier. If the guys behind you can catch the ball, pitching to contact never goes out of style.

Musial doubled in the top of the second, but he was stranded. In the bottom of the second, Broglio got back to pounding the bottom of the zone. Rocky Nelson led off with a single—and was eliminated when Cimoli hit a comebacker for a 1-6-3 double play. Smoky Burgess picked up the third Pittsburgh hit but didn't advance as Don Hoak hit into a force play to end the inning.

Broglio had given up three base hits, but no Pirate had even reached second base. But with another 1-2-3 for his teammates in the third, Broglio knew he was in for a battle. Bill Mazeroski led off the Pittsburgh third by singling, and moved to third on a sac bunt and a fly out. But Groat hit one back to Broglio for the third out, and the game stayed tied.

"I focused on me and the catcher, and the location of the ball," he recalls. "I really didn't think about how the ballgame went. I knew that it was a low-scoring game, but other than that, all I wanted to do was focus and make sure that we didn't give up too many hits or walks or whatever else to get beat in that ballgame."

Friend continued to upstage Broglio by the slightest margin in the middle innings. He dispensed with the Nos. 2-3-4 hitters in the St. Louis lineup in the fourth. Then Skinner benefited from a rare miscue by the Cardinals defense, reaching base to open the bottom of the fourth on a Javier error. Nelson flied out for the first out.

Recognizing the tight nature of the game, the Pirates put on a play with No. 5 hitter Cimoli. It didn't work. Cimoli struck out, and Skinner was thrown out trying to take second on the play. Musial, Walt Moryn, and Carl Sawatski went down in order in the fifth, and the game was scoreless at the halfway mark. Or rather, at the halfway point of a regulation game. On this night, though, the two clubs and the two pitchers were still just getting started.

The Pirates finally broke through in the fifth against Broglio.

Burgess led off with a home run, the first run of the game. Hoak followed with a single, the first consecutive baserunners against Broglio, and the first time Broglio was in anything like trouble. So, of course, Broglio collected another double play, this one going 6-3 off the bat of Bill Mazeroski. One more ground out and he was out of the fifth. Every time his defense made a play behind him, Broglio locked down even more.

"What it does is make you believe that what you start, you're going to finish," he says. "Because it's going to be a low-scoring ballgame. We had a good-hitting ballclub along with defense, but we had a lot of close ballgames. And that's what makes you want to pitch even harder."

Typically, Broglio was not known for his control. He was among the league leaders in walks allowed in four different seasons, and he issued 100 free passes in 1960—the third-highest total in the National League. But against the Pirates he had no such troubles. He didn't walk a single batter all night, allowing him to keep plugging away. It's the first thing he mentions when the game is brought up. He pitched deep into the game, he pitched well, and the Cardinals won. First in Broglio's mind, though, is the zero in the walk column.

"We committed one error, but when both pitchers pitch in a ballgame where there's no walks, you know you've either got good defense or we made some great pitches," Broglio says.

He made even more great pitches after the fifth. Hoak's single was the last baserunner against Broglio for a long, long time. Both clubs went in order in the sixth, with Broglio striking out Virdon and Groat in the bottom half of the inning. Groat struck out 35 times in 1960 en route to an MVP season. More than 10 percent of those Ks came against Broglio on one night.

"I was very lucky that day with Dick Groat," Broglio admits. "Because Dick Groat normally made a lot of contact with the ball. But that particular day I think I struck him out four times. And three of those times he got caught taking the pitch. So that particular day I had my curveball, slider, and fastball located very well."

The seventh whizzed by just like the sixth, with a pair of 1-2-3's. Nelson grounded out, Cimoli hit a liner to right, and Burgess grounded out. It was eight in a row and counting for Broglio. Although he still trailed by a run, he was breezing. And in the eighth he was let off the hook.

Moryn's one-out triple keyed the inning, and Sawatski's RBI single scored pinch runner Charlie James. Flood struck out, bringing up Broglio, and the pitcher drew the only walk issued in the entire game. The inning ended when pinch hitter George Crowe struck out, but Broglio got a boost just from being on base.

"A lot of times in my career, if I had a chance to bat in the latter part of the ballgame, I caught a second wind for some reason or other," Broglio explains. "I don't know whether it was the way I worked or what, but I always caught a second wind. A lot of the time, the seventh inning was like the first inning for me. There were ballgames I lost 12 pounds in 90-degree heat and 90-percent humidity, but I finished the ballgame."

And as this game wore on, Broglio grew more and more convinced that he was going to finish it too. The problem was, it was also growing more likely that nine innings would not be enough to register the complete game. Broglio once again got the shutdown, which many pitchers consider the most important part of the game. After his offense got him a run, he didn't give it back. He struck out Hoak, then got a couple of outs in the air. He'd put down 11 in a row, meeting Friend's challenge.

"It's like on a golf course, if you've got a guy that's playing real well, you want to play as well as he is," Broglio says. "If he's playing bad, maybe he might take his game to you if he starts not making the shots. I knew I was going to face tough pitchers, and I wanted to make sure I was competitive in that respect."

Musial nearly delivered the game-winner in regulation. Following a two-out single in the ninth by Boyer, Musial doubled to right. Boyer motored around, trying to score on the play, but he was thrown out at the plate. If Broglio was going to get the win, he would be working overtime.

First, though, he had to make it to extras. Another perfect frame, this time against Virdon, Groat, and Skinner, made it 14 straight and forced extra innings. But Friend kept matching him zero for zero, keeping the Cardinals off the board in the top of the 10th. Broglio twirled a perfect 10th, bringing the total to 17 straight outs. As for the 11th? More of the same. Two teams, two pitchers, six batters, six outs. Broglio's streak reached 20 consecutive outs, and he saw no reason he couldn't go all night.

That is, until Musial's spot in the batting order came around again. White rapped a leadoff single in the 12th, and Boyer flied out to bring up "Stan the Man." Musial was exactly the man the Cardinals wanted up in such a situation, even at age 39.

"That's a short porch in right field at the old Forbes Field," Broglio recalls. "And him being a left-handed hitter against a right-handed pitcher, you were happy to see him. Either him or Bill White—any left-handed hitter. But Stan being who he is, and in his home area, both ways it was great."

And of course the legend delivered. Musial cranked a two-run home run, giving Broglio his first lead of the night. Broglio would have been delighted to get the help from anyone, but from Musial it was doubly sweet.

"He hit the home run," Broglio says, "and I wanted to take him out for a cocktail. And he said, 'No, I'm going to take care of you. Don't worry about it.' I said, 'You won the ballgame,' and he said, 'You pitched a heck of a ballgame.' That's the type of guy he was. He complimented you on things you did."

Before the celebration, though, there was the matter of getting the last three outs. They were, without a doubt, the hardest outs of the game for Broglio. He caught a third wind, now admitting that he was probably too excited when he started the 12th.

"The adrenaline was really flowing, because I really wanted to complete the game," he says. "You get 12 innings in, and pitch the way Bob Friend and I did, then you want to finish it. It maybe pumped me up a little bit, but I didn't give in. Sometimes that happens. Nowadays, you've got a game like that going, you're out of there. They don't give you that opportunity to finish."

With the chance at a 12-inning complete-game win against the league leaders, who wouldn't be pretty psyched? But Broglio had to rein it in, or he was in danger of being removed. As hard as everyone had worked, manager Johnny Keane wasn't going to let Broglio give the game away.

Virdon singled to lead off the 12th, snapping Broglio's streak at 20 straight outs. Broglio had to collect himself, and he did. He struck out Groat one more time, and Skinner grounded out, advancing Virdon to second. Two down, tying run at the plate. One out away, but out No. 36 was a grind. Nelson doubled, scoring Virdon and slicing the St. Louis lead to a single run. The tying run was now in scoring position, and the winning run was at the plate in the form of the very dangerous pinch hitter, Dick Stuart.

"The way we looked at it was: what we started is what we want to finish," Broglio says. "I'm thinking about finishing a ballgame that I thought was a heck of a ballgame. I didn't want to give it to [reliever] Lindy McDaniel. And if Bob Friend went up on me, he did not want to give it to [reliever] Elroy Face."

Keane stuck with Broglio against the menacing presence of Stuart, who had hit 27 homers the year before and finished 1960 with 23 more. Broglio knew Stuart could hurt him, but he also knew he could get the slugger out. And on this occasion, good pitching did in fact stifle good hitting. Stuart struck out, and Broglio had his victory—and his complete game. The Pirates went on to win the pennant, and then the World Series. But Broglio had a treasured memory, one he still holds on to.

He has an inscribed game ball from the night, with the particulars of the game detailed on it. But he may not need the reminder of his biggest game.

"I've got a couple balls, but that's the one that stands out," he says. "I don't even have my 20th win, which I pitched against the Giants—who traded me to the Cardinals. That was my 20th victory. But this game here . . . I always talk about this game."

CHAPTER 9

MARK WHITEN

There was no career minor league catcher named Crash Davis. Ebby Calvin "Nuke" LaLoosh may resemble plenty of young pitchers, but he's no more than a fictional character. There's one real player, however, whose name appears in the wonderful baseball movie *Bull Durham*. It's Mark Whiten—at the time a highly drafted outfield prospect in the Toronto Blue Jays farm system. Whiten never met Davis, LaLoosh, or Annie Savoy.

At one point in the film, the minor league players are riding on a bus from one Carolina League port of call to another. Davis, the veteran catcher, is reading *Baseball America*. LaLoosh, the hotshot pitching prospect approaches Davis in hopes of gleaning some wisdom about the game. In the shot of the magazine, a headline is visible:

"Hard-Hittin' Whiten"

They had no idea how right they were.

Whiten himself was a Class A player at the time, just like the fictional Bulls, and in fact he wasn't stationed all that far away from Durham. He was in his second professional season, playing for Myrtle Beach of the South Atlantic League, in the Blue Jays organization. The Sally League is a rank below the Carolina League, but it's certainly pretty close.

Whiten saw *Bull Durham* in theaters—what baseball player or fan didn't?—but he didn't catch his "cameo." It's rather brief, and you can miss it if you don't know to look for it. Some of Whiten's Myrtle Beach teammates did see it, however, and they told him about it. He grabbed a copy of the magazine, something he still holds on to 20 years later.

"That's something that's cool to me," he says. "Guys told me about it. I went to see the movie and I didn't even see it. But later on, I saw it on the video. That was cool."

There's another parallel. Like Davis, who set the career minor league home run record before finally retiring, Whiten had his moment. His name is not only in *Baseball America*, it's in the record books for a mark that may one day be tied but is unlikely to ever be broken.

On September 7, 1993, Whiten became the 12th player in major league history to hit four home runs in a game. Three have equaled the feat since, bringing the total to 15. He also drove in 12 runs in the game, tying him with "Sunny" Jim Bottomley for the all-time record. Whiten was always a hard hitter, a big guy who could rip a ball a mile when he got the barrel of the bat on one. He didn't always harness his raw power and translate it into extra bases, but he was a productive ballplayer for more than a decade.

He played in 11 major league seasons, hit 105 home runs and drove in 423 runs. But on one night in 1993, he put it all together and was the hardest hitter in baseball. To many fans, the power surge is all Whiten is remembered for, but he's got no qualms about that. He just figures it's nice to be remembered at all.

"It doesn't really bother me," he says. "I just take it as it comes. To me, I had a great career. Baseball was very good to me. It provided a nice home life for me. I just take it for what it is. If somebody wants to talk about it, I'll talk about it. It isn't something I'm going to bring up, but if somebody calls me and asks me about it, I try to give the best answer I can."

Whiten says things like that a lot. He takes things as they come and doesn't try to change what he knows he can't. It's impressive for a man whose big-league career ended before he was ready for it to be over. His last major league game came in May of 2000, six months before his 34th birthday. His last season with more than eight games

---

"Hard Hittin'" Mark Whiten made baseball history in the second game of a doubleheader at old Riverfront Stadium. *AP/WWP*

played was two years before that. Whiten felt he was a better hitter as he got older, but he didn't get the chance to show it off. He finally hung it up, and now his only real contact with the game is helping teach it to his son.

"In '96, I learned how to hit the ball a little bit better," he says. "But when I learned how to hit, that's when the jobs started getting slim. Earlier in my career, I wasn't that good of a hitter. I was just big and strong, with some idea. But I learned how to be more consistent with my swing and take a better approach."

After a life in the majors, he admits it was difficult to put what he needed to put into playing in the independent leagues. Whiten took more than 3,000 major league at-bats, and called such cathedrals as Yankee Stadium, Fenway Park, and Busch Stadium home. Somehow, playing for the Long Island Ducks didn't drive him in the same way as wearing the "birds on the bat" or the famous pinstripes.

"In independent ball, it was hard for me to get up for some of the games," he says. "I look back at it, and you've got to make yourself get motivated to play when it's time to go. I had no problems walking away from it. I still enjoy the game. I've got my kid now that I'm trying to help learn the game."

On his way through the minors, Whiten wasn't actually a big-time power prospect. He hit some home runs, 10-15 a year, but not by the truckload. He was, however, always patient. He drew plenty of walks, and he struck out a lot as well. Whiten saw plenty of deep counts—and it was more of the same when he reached the majors. Whiten always posted solid on-base percentages, but his power didn't emerge until '93, when he joined the Cardinals.

That spring, St. Louis acquired Whiten from Cleveland for Juan Andujar and Mark Clark. The Cards were already his third big-league team, and he was only 26. But the National League suited him, and Whiten started to take advantage of his power potential. He had 11 home runs at the All-Star break, and cranked four more in his first seven games of the second half. Whiten, who frequently tweaked and tinkered with his swing, was able to stay relatively stable with his stroke. It added up to a breakthrough year.

"That particular year I was pretty much consistent with the same thing," he says. "The big thing for me was learning how to get my weight back, and stay back. When I did that, that's when I had success."

However, he was slumping when the Redbirds hit Cincinnati in early September for a doubleheader. Whiten hadn't gone deep since August 11, a stretch of nearly four weeks. A twinbill on artificial turf isn't typically a struggling player's first choice for how to get sorted out, though. And in the opener, Whiten looked every bit like a player in a funk. He was one of few Cardinals not to have a big showing in Game 1, going 0-for-4 with a bases-loaded walk in the 14-13 loss. His teammates amassed 17 hits, but Whiten couldn't even get one. There was no reason to expect anything extraordinary in the night game, either.

"It was just a typical day," Whiten says. "Usually we would get up around noon, I'd try to eat lunch and my routine was to go to the ballpark early instead of sitting around the room."

So by first pitch of the nightcap, Whiten had already been at work for 10 hours. It was a now-rare true doubleheader, with both games played under the lights. The second contest didn't get started until 9:46 p.m. eastern time.

Whiten got going quickly, though. Geronimo Pena drew a lead-off walk against starter Larry Luebbers, but was forced at second when Lonnie Maclin hit a grounder to short. Bernard Gilkey flied out, but Todd Zeile drew a walk to keep the inning alive. Gerald Perry's single loaded the bases, bringing up Whiten. Having gone 27 days without a long ball, Whiten assuredly was not thinking "dinger." The switch-hitter swung from the left side against the right-hander Luebbers.

"I was just trying to get a run home, basically," he says. "That was it. The goal is to try to get the run home. I just wanted to connect to one in the left-center gap. I learned that if I took that approach all the time, I might have been a lot better hitter. It makes you stay on the ball a whole lot better. It's hard to do on a consistent basis, but usually when I was hitting well, that was my focus no matter what the pitch was. If I stayed to that left-center gap trying to drive the ball that way, I was more consistent."

He drove it, all right, and it went just where he wanted—left-center. Starter Bob Tewksbury and the Cardinals had a 4-0 lead, thanks in large part to the lead Whiten had. He got ahead in the count, 3-0, and crushed a get-me-over pitch from Luebbers.

"The big thing about getting ahead is trying to stay relaxed and still make that good swing without going too far out of the strike zone," he said. "That day, that's what I did."

Cincinnati got two back in the bottom of the first, but from there the game mercifully quieted down a bit. Following the 27-run insanity earlier in the evening, a few goose eggs on the board were welcome. Whiten popped up in the top of the fourth, and a Maclin sacrifice fly in the fifth made it a 5-2 St. Louis lead. The game was more than half over by the time Whiten got his next at-bat.

But in the sixth, against reliever Mike Anderson, Whiten resumed his unwitting charge toward a record. Anderson walked Zeile and Perry, bringing up Whiten, and the usually patient hitter mixed things up. Knowing Anderson would want to come over the plate after two free passes, Whiten pounced on the first pitch he saw from the right-hander. And he drilled it, this time to right-center, for his second homer and fifth, sixth, and seventh RBIs.

"You can't try to hit a home run," he insists. "That day, I didn't try to hit home runs. I just happened to connect for home runs. I can only think of two occasions when I tried and actually did it. But those are far and few between. When you try, you usually pop up or miss."

Anderson was still the pitcher in the seventh, but this time he put down the first two batters. However, Gilkey, Zeile, and Perry all singled, stretching the inning and the lead and giving Whiten another chance to hit. Whiten remembers the pitch sequence with great clarity. He proudly points out that he swung at only six pitches all game, and four of them left the yard.

"He threw a ball, threw a curveball and I fouled it off, and then he threw another ball," he recounts. "Then he threw a fastball and that was another swing." And another home run: Cards 12, Reds 2. By now Whiten had 10 ribbies, already rare air in the history of the game. He'd also reached the power hitter's single-game standard, the three-homer game. Four is something hitters don't even dare think about. For sluggers, though, three is attainable.

"I was more excited about the third one than the fourth one," Whiten says. "I had never hit three in a game. So that was more exciting."

For the eighth, the Reds called on Rob Dibble to pitch mop-up. Dibble had fallen off drastically since his prime as one of the "Nasty

Boys" in the Reds bullpen. His control had vanished, as he walked more than a batter per inning in '93. Mind you, that's still not a fun at-bat. He still had some juice on his fastball, and it can be even more uncomfortable when a pitcher throws hard but can't quite control where it goes. But Whiten knew the book on Dibble.

"All you had to do was look for the fastball," he recalls. "He wasn't that tough, like he was back when he was throwing a 95-mph slider for a strike. He was just trying to get some work in, which is when a guy is likely to lay something in there. But also, the way I was locked in, it may not have even mattered."

That much is surely true. And when Dibble put himself in a fastball count, the odds swung even more in favor of the hitter. Facing a 2-0 count, Whiten knew he was likely to get the heater. Sitting dead red, he swung and connected for the historic homer—a two-run blast that scored Perry.

"I remember when I was going up to bat, the batboy saying, 'Are you going to try to hit another home run?' I said, 'I didn't try to hit the other three, so why should I try to hit another one?' That's all I remember. I just got up there and tried to put a good swing, and it happened."

Four home runs, 12 RBIs, and a big win. It was pretty much a perfect night, except that the second game didn't come to an end until past midnight. And though it was after deadline in many newspaper markets, Whiten was in demand for the rest of the night.

"I remember going back to the hotel," he says. "I called the wife, and I had to put a block on the phone because reporters just started calling. And it was already one o'clock in the morning."

When Whiten looks back on the game, there's no temptation to romanticize it or imbue it with some sort of magic. He looks at the pitches, looks at the swings, recalls his approach, and it all adds up.

"It was more just the pitchers missing their spots," he admits. "I look at replays sometimes, and they miss their spots by a couple inches and that's the difference. If he'd hit his spot, I might not have hit the ball. I look at the highlights, and every time he missed by an inch or two, enough for me to get good wood on it."

The humility is impressive, but by the same token, there have been many more than 15 games when pitchers made mistakes. On Whiten's end, he believes his key was staying with the ball. He got in trouble when he got pull-happy.

Even more impressive, and more surprising, is that Whiten stayed hot in the coming days. Mike Cameron hit four home runs in May of 2002, then hit .184 with one long ball in his next 103 at-bats. Bob Horner cracked four in July of 1986, and followed it up with a 20-for-97 (.206), one-homer skid. It doesn't happen to everyone, but it does happen. For Whiten, though, the game propelled him to more success. He hit .327 and slugged .577 over the next 14 games, allowing him to flirt with the 100-RBI mark.

"I knew if I just tried to stay consistent and tried to drive the ball to left-center, I would have a better chance of having success," he says. "I never thought about hitting home runs a lot. I talked to some guys who did try, and I'm like, 'I can't do that, man. I'd make an out every time.'"

In the end, Whiten came up just short of triple figures, totaling 99 RBIs on the year.

"I was trying," he says. "I don't think it was meant to happen. I'd be on deck, Todd Zeile would be up, first and second, and he'd hit into a double play, and I'd make the third out. We must have done that five or six times. It never worked out."

It would be his most productive season in terms of counting numbers, as he set personal bests in homers (25), RBIs, runs (81), and total bases (238). However, it wasn't his most effective season. That was still to come.

Whiten spent all of the strike-shortened '94 season with the Cardinals, but he was traded to Boston before the '95 campaign. That was a short stay, and in July he was on the move again, this time to Philadelphia. A slow start to '96 earned Whiten his release from the Phillies, but he wasn't done. He was about to start his finest stretch as a major league hitter.

After receiving his release from the Phils, Whiten signed on with the Braves. And it was in Atlanta that he found something he wished he'd found years earlier. When Whiten was 29, the light switch finally flipped on. But his timing couldn't have been worse.

"Their hitting instructor, Clarence Jones, taught me to shorten my swing and hit the ball hard," he says. "A couple of other coaches taught me some things as well, but he said a couple things that really stuck with me and related to my swing. And all of a sudden, the ball started jumping off my bat a lot better without me making that hard, aggressive swing, over-swinging. Then I got traded. They had to make room for some guy named Andruw Jones. So I had to go. Some kid."

Whiten laughs at the unfortunate coincidence, which suits him better than bitterness. He missed out on a trip to the World Series, but it's hard to argue with Atlanta's decision to find a spot for the young player who made five All-Star teams and won 10 Gold Gloves as a Brave.

The good news is that he took what he learned in Atlanta and applied it with a vengeance in Seattle. In 140 at-bats as a Mariner, Whiten cranked 12 home runs, hit .300, and slugged .607. In the words of Crash Davis, "That's a career, man. In any league."

"I started swinging the bat real well and I ended up playing pretty much the whole time," Whiten says. "The ball just started jumping off my bat. I was impressing myself with some of the balls I was hitting. I think '96 was the best year I had hitting-wise, when I was in Seattle. If you look at the numbers, the numbers speak for themselves.

"Not only the numbers, but just the way that I was hitting the ball at the time is what stands out to me more than anything. The numbers say what they say, but if you saw some of the balls I hit, you'd be like, 'Dang, where did that come from?' I know I was!"

And yet within two years, his time as a full-time big leaguer was over. He played more games at Triple-A Buffalo than with Cleveland in 1999, and again in 2000. He made brief returns to action at Triple-A Las Vegas in 2002 and Long Island in '03, but just as Whiten was starting to figure things out, his career was basically over.

"That's just the way it goes," he says. "It seems like when you get better, that's when the opportunities get slimmer. But it was a good time for me."

Whiten's only regret is that he wishes that light had come on earlier. But true to form, he doesn't dwell on it. He controlled what he could control, and the game gave him a good life.

"Without a doubt, I wish it had," he said. "But I played the hand that I was dealt. If I could go back and change it, yeah, maybe. But I just take it for what it is and leave it at that."

CHAPTER 10

AL HRABOSKY

As a player and as a broadcaster, Al Hrabosky has never been the sort who suits everyone. He was demonstrative on the mound and occasionally abrasive toward authority figures in the clubhouse. For plenty of fans, that made him a hero. For some, it made him a love-to-hate kind of player. But as Hrabosky surely understands, now that he calls Cardinals games on television, either option is good. Love you or hate you, as long as they're talking about you, it's just fine.

That was part of the problem for Hrabosky in 1975. For one of the few times in his career and his life, he was under the radar. But the fans of St. Louis and the Cardinals organization came to his defense, leading to one of the more memorable promotions at Busch Stadium and Hrabosky's favorite day from his playing career.

Entering the All-Star break in '75, Hrabosky led the National League in saves with 14. He carried a spiffy 1.80 ERA, had a 5-2 record and had permitted one home run all season. It was difficult for a reliever to make the All-Star team in the '70s. Only two bullpenners were on the National League roster in '75. But Hrabosky felt he had a legitimate case, and so did Cardinals fans and management. He was having an excellent year, racking up saves and innings despite a rough year for the club.

Yet because Dodgers manager—and National League All-Star manager—Walter Alston didn't think to look him up, Hrabosky was an oversight when it came to All-Star selections.

"I was not selected for the '75 All-Star team, and everybody was all upset," Hrabosky says, "But things were so different then. You did-n't have *SportsCenter* and those deals. It was just an honest thing. You didn't have the decision making like you do today. When everyone complained that I didn't make it, [Alston] said, 'Well, what kind of season is he having? He isn't even listed in the Sunday statistics.'"

That in itself shows the difference in eras. Before Internet stats, even before the weekly Tuesday and Wednesday team-by-team stats rundowns in *USA Today*, the only consistent source for baseball statistics was the Sunday newspaper. And pitchers only made the listings if they had a certain number of decisions. Hrabosky was 3-2 when the selections were made, and he was left off the squad. It did not go over well in St. Louis.

"He picked Mike Marshall, who was his Cy Young Award winner from the year before, and Tug McGraw," Hrabosky says. "But both of them were having subpar years. I was leading the league in saves, had a winning record and an ERA under 2. They had less saves than me combined, and higher ERAs."

So St. Louis fandom galvanized behind its colorful reliever. With Alston's Dodgers coming to town for the last series before the All-Star break, the Cardinals held the "We Hlove Hrabosky Hbanner Hday" in honor of the man known as the "Mad Hungarian." The club offered free admission to the Saturday game for anyone who brought a banner—sorry, a Hbanner—backing Hrabosky. It was a raging success. The announced, paid attendance was 31,606, but Hrabosky asserts that there were at least 50,000 people actually in the seats.

"Jerry Lovelace was our PR director, and he kind of mentioned something to me," Hrabosky says. "He said, 'This is terrible. We're going to have to do something to protest this.' And he came up with the Hbanner Hday. I was flattered, but I remember saying, 'Do whatever you want, but do not make it look like I'm the one complaining.' And I remember getting dressed after the conversation, and I came back upstairs and I said, 'Well, what happens if nobody shows up?' And he goes, 'Trust me.'"

He was right. Hrabosky had no reason to worry.

Al Hrabosky was known as a colorful, demonstrative player, and those same traits apply to his style as a television commentator. *AP/WWP*

"It was a day we didn't take batting practice," Hrabosky says. "I went out on the field to run and all that, and there was this thunderous ovation and all these banners. And it was like, we have all these great players, but they never had a Hbanner Hday."

For a player who thrived on crowd interactions, it was a perfect day. Hrabosky loved the reactions he got from the fans when he played. With a stadium full of people supporting him, Hrabosky was able to dig even deeper. For some, baseball is all about controlling and limiting your emotions. For Hrabosky, it was about inflaming them and harnessing the energy. So a full stadium of Mad Hungarian fans brought out the best in him.

"I always tried to create a one-on-one battle with the hitter," he says. "So if he stepped out or anything like that, it just fueled the energy level. In that case, I said to myself, 'OK, you're out there all by yourself and you want this, you think you're good enough, you better show why you're good enough, and don't let these people down who came out here to support you.' So I always tried to use those kinds of things as motivation."

However, he insists that his famous histrionics weren't for the fans—they were for himself. Hrabosky had an elaborate psych-up act that he did behind the mound, getting himself fully pumped up.

"At the All-Star break in '74, I came up with this idea of going behind the mound and doing all that stuff. It was all designed to help me. It was done for myself, and I really turned it around. I had a stretch in the second half where I was virtually unhittable, and then '75 got off to a good start and it just kind of carried over."

As a competitor and an entertainer, Hrabosky had a line to walk. He came up in the Cardinals organization, and he was taught the importance of a respect for the game and for your opponent. He made it a point not to show opponents up. But that's a difficult distinction to make at times. It can be tough to identify where getting yourself psyched up ends and taunting the opponent begins. Hrabosky admits that the act didn't always go over well with the other side.

"Obviously the opposition, it ticked them off," he admits now. "But it seems like some of the guys I had the biggest confrontations with, after our careers were over, at old-timers games and stuff, they were the first ones to come up and say, 'Hey, are you going to do something special?'"

He emphasizes the difference between his performances and those of some of his spiritual heirs.

"You started seeing some of the gyrations of some of the guys, but my thing was always done beforehand," he says. "If I got you out, I just went on to the next guy. I didn't really do anything [to taunt]. I think they appreciated the competitiveness. They didn't like it, but in hindsight they look back and say, 'He wasn't trying to show me up.' Now, you hit a home run, a guy flips a bat."

The distinctions got even more subtle because Hrabosky really did relish the showmanship aspect of his job. He knew something in the '70s that many other athletes didn't realize until a decade or two later: if someone buys a ticket to see you play, you're an entertainer.

"I kind of thrived on it," he says. "Because I felt like if I could have 50,000 people in the palm of my hand, they weren't going to react until I did something. At times I felt like I could kind of manipulate the crowd a little bit. It was fun to have the recognition. Even the people that hated me, they were like, 'I hate you, but I sure hope you pitch.' Now, they probably hoped that I got shellacked, but still . . ."

Hrabosky didn't get shellacked on his special day. In fact, he couldn't have scripted it any better than it turned out. With the Cardinals trailing 1-0, he entered the game in the top of the ninth to face the sixth, seventh, and eighth hitters in the Dodgers order. He struck out Ron Cey, got Bill Russell to ground out, and got Steve Yeager to fly out, keeping the deficit at a single run.

Given one last chance, the Cardinals took advantage. Reggie Smith led off the ninth with a homer against starter Al Downing, and what do you know, Alston called on his All-Star Marshall to pitch the remainder of the inning. Marshall escaped without incident, and the game went to extras.

Marshall was removed after only one inning for pinch hitter Lee Lacy, whom Hrabosky put down with a 6-3 groundout. Davey Lopes flied to center, and Tom Paciorek grounded to second. Hrabosky went six up, six down on his day, and he put it in his offense's hands to try to get him a win. They delivered. Ken Reitz singled and moved to second when Mike Tyson sacrificed. Bake McBride poked a one-out RBI single to center, ending the game in a Cardinals victory.

"I won, and then I won on Sunday," Hrabosky recalls. "And [shortly] after the All-Star break, we went out and played the Dodgers and I won the first game there too. So I kind of felt like we got the point across. He figured out who I was at that point."

Decisions weren't a problem again all year for the left-hander. Hrabosky secured an almost unheard-of six relief wins in a seven-appearance stretch from July 12–25. He finished the year with 13 wins to go along with 22 saves, leading the National League. Hrabosky placed third in the Cy Young balloting that year and eighth in the MVP vote—after being left off the All-Star team.

Hrabosky never did hear from Alston, but again, it was a different time. There weren't five different shows on cable breaking down the decisions on the All-Star roster. And neither player nor manager carried a cell phone or pager with him at all times. That also may have made it easier for Hrabosky himself to deal with the slight. Not to mention the fact that the breather was always welcome for a relief pitcher.

"It would have been nice, but it was never my focal point," he says. "At that point, I usually needed the three days off. Back then, you pitched more, but more importantly, from the seventh inning on, you got up. If you were behind by a run or two, or you were even, or you were ahead, you got a lefty and a righty up. You'd throw two or three innings and not get in the game."

He still remembers some of the banners, and he has one of them in his house today. One read, "Smog isn't the densest thing in L.A." Another featured an image of Hrabosky with the words, "Support your local flamethrower." In a strange coincidence, Hrabosky bought a house in the St. Louis area in 1993, and the person selling the house to him and his wife had that very banner stored away. She passed it on to the new owners, and now Hrabosky has a unique reminder of his playing days. Anybody can have a jersey or a ball or a bat. They don't all have banners.

As Hrabosky's career went on, though, he became a more controversial figure. His showmanship didn't always even sit well with the home fans, never mind folks who were partial toward the Cardinals opponents. And then there were the issues within his own clubhouse. Following a disappointing 1976 campaign, the Cardinals parted with iconic manager Red Schoendienst, replacing him with Vern Rapp, a stern figure to contrast with laissez-faire Schoendienst.

"Vern Rapp came in as a disciplinarian," Hrabosky explains. "Red got fired because Keith Hernandez and Templeton and these guys came in. I grew up under [Bob] Gibson and [Lou] Brock and [Tim] McCarver and [Joe] Torre, and even [Steve] Carlton was there my first year. And they taught us that you play the game hard, then go have your fun. Baseball was first and foremost.

"It seemed like those guys came up, and the game got in the way of their social life. It took them a while to learn. Red treated you like a man. And those guys kind of ultimately got him fired. Then they bring in Vern Rapp, who deserved a shot, but he'd gotten to a level where he couldn't cope."

One of Rapp's acts was to ban long hair and facial hair, a decision that put him in direct conflict with Hrabosky, who had both long hair on the back of his head and a Fu Manchu on his face.

"When the hair-and-mustache issue came up with Rapp, there were people who maybe didn't like the long hair, but it was never an issue before," Hrabosky recalls. "So now, they forced them to make a decision one way or another. People liked me, and now all of a sudden I want to take a stand, now I'm a bad guy? It became a situation where, if two batboys got in a fight, it was over that.

"The *Post-Dispatch* ran a 'hair-o-meter,' my record with hair and without hair. It was a definite personality clash between the two of us. It didn't affect that many people initially, but then it grew as the season went along. I'm man enough to say I wish I could have handled things differently. At times I kind of egged things on."

Rapp outlasted Hrabosky, but not by much. Hrabosky was traded to Kansas City in December of '77, while Rapp was fired after 17 games in '78. Hrabosky played on two playoff teams after leaving St. Louis, with the Royals in '78 and the Braves in '82—the latter team facing the Cardinals in the National League Championship Series.

Upon retirement, though, he was back in St. Louis. He moved into the broadcast booth in 1985, and has been a television voice for the Redbirds ever since. He's even opened a bar right outside Busch Stadium, where fans can see mementos of his playing career—and occasionally see the man himself. He's not nearly so controversial these days, unless you count fan disputes over whether he strikes the right tone in calling games. But even when that's the case, the same old thing holds true: at least they don't forget him.

CHAPTER 11

BOB TEWKSBURY

Bob Tewksbury didn't exactly rocket through the minor leagues, even on his first try. He underwent elbow surgery as a prospect in the Yankees system. He also fought an ingrained bias against pitchers who don't throw hard. The combination of health and velocity issues slowed Tewksbury's march to baseball's most hallowed grounds. If the first climb was slow, though, Tewksbury's subsequent quests to reach "The Show" were utterly interminable. He would get a cup of coffee here and a September call-up there, but that was all he had to show for season after season, toiling in the minors.

Drafted in the 19th round in 1981, Tewksbury played in the bus leagues for nearly five years before his first taste of major league life. When you rely on craft and command, it's harder to catch the eyes of the decision makers. And when you don't have the pedigree as a high-round draft pick, it's even tougher. Yet when Tewksbury made the majors, he showed he belonged. As a rookie, Tewksbury went 9-5 for the 1986 Yankees, posting a sharp 3.31 ERA. He kept the ball in the park and threw strikes—the hallmarks of his pitching throughout his career.

Even then, he wasn't a power pitcher—49 strikeouts in 130⅓ innings tell that story. But he could crack 90 miles an hour once in a while; it wasn't total junk. And there was never any doubt that the New Hampshire native had a plan and an idea on the mound.

"I think I always had it," he said. "I knew how to pitch. One of my biggest assets was game awareness, and being able to pitch."

After that extended stretch in the New York rotation, Tewksbury might well have expected that he was set. He'd proved himself in the American League. He was a big leaguer to stay, it seemed.

He would have been wrong. The next time Tewksbury got an extended run in the majors, the year was 1990—four years, a trade, another arm operation, and two organizations later. And even that chance almost didn't happen. In 1987, Tewksbury started slow with the Yankees as he tried to pitch through shoulder soreness. He was traded to the Cubs as part of a package for Steve Trout, but went 0-4 with a 6.50 ERA with Chicago after the deal. He made one big-league start in 1988, but shoulder surgery finally sidelined him.

"As a young player I was scared to death of getting sent down, worrying about my place on the team," he said. "Sometimes you pitch to that fear, and it happens. When I got traded to the Cubs, I was hurt. I had a sore shoulder, and I still was trying to battle those fears of performance. But I was also hurt."

Tewksbury came back from injury and found himself with even less zip on his fastball than he had before. Fortunately, he didn't have to relearn his way of pitching, since he never blew anyone away in the first place. But it meant that in order to make his mark, he'd have to be even better than before. The chances would be fewer and further between, and the margin for error even slimmer.

So for 1989 it was another year and another organization. Tewksbury signed a minor league deal with the Cardinals. He viewed himself as a big leaguer, but the Cardinals saw him more as depth for the farm system. He earned a late-season call-up after a year at Triple-A Louisville, and fared well.

"They took a shot," he said. "When I was pitching well in Louisville, the Cardinals needed a starting pitcher. Whitey [Herzog] has told me, he said, 'Your name came up, but I didn't think you threw hard enough. I just didn't think that you could pitch.' We joke about it. He said, 'You proved me wrong.'"

Yet Tewksbury still couldn't lock in as a full-time St. Louis starter. After making that good impression in '89, Tewksbury was hurt more

---

It took Bob Tewksbury what seemed like forever to establish himself, but once he settled in Tewksbury was a productive big leaguer for a long time. *AP/WWP*

than some by the labor strife in the winter of '89–'90. Baseball endured its seventh work stoppage in less than two decades, with a lockout erasing much of Spring Training. It was in the spring that Tewksbury would have had the chance to build on his 1989 showing. Instead, he sat on the sidelines, waiting and thinking. And he started to consider more dramatic options.

"The lockout happens and I'm back in Louisville again," he said. "I'm thinking, 'I'm going to go to Japan and play. I'm tired of this. I've been up and down seven times with three different organizations.'"

Fortunately, he resisted the temptation. Tewksbury made the Cardinals out of Spring Training, but as a reliever, not a starter. After eight bullpen appearances it was back to the minors, but in June he got one more chance. And he pounced on it.

It was that one game, one night in mid-June that showed Tewksbury he belonged, that showed him he could do the work at baseball's highest level. Tewksbury took a make-or-break moment and made it rather than breaking. Tewksbury got a one-start shot for the Cardinals at home against Montreal. He'd been toiling at Louisville, looking for the time when he'd finally receive not just a start or two but the opportunity to stick in somebody's rotation for a while.

When he was called up in mid-June, a chance like that was exactly what was on the table. A straight-shooting former catcher told him what was at stake.

"I remember Ted Simmons was the director of player development at that time," Tewskbury said. "And when he brought me up, outside the locker room he said, 'Look. You're going to get the ball on Saturday night against the Expos. You're up here to see what you can do. If you do well, you'll get the ball again. If you don't, I don't know. There are no guarantees.' So I was scared to death. That's what players long to hear, the hard truth, and it scared the hell out of me. But at the same time, I knew where I stood."

He held Montreal off the board for four innings before the Expos tallied three times in the fifth. But in the bottom half of that inning, St. Louis got two runs back. In the sixth they tied it up. In the bottom of the seventh, Craig Wilson pinch hit for the pitcher, and his single sparked a go-ahead two-run rally. Tewksbury, of course, was still the pitcher of record, and he picked up his first big-league win of the year. With one start, he equaled his major league win total from the previous three seasons combined.

"I remember driving to the ballpark the night of the game against the Expos totally confident, totally calm," Tewksbury said. "And I pitched seven innings with [three runs], I got the win, and of course I got the ball five days later. That snowballed into a chance for me to play into a position in the major leagues."

A week later, Tewksbury did the one thing that endears you more to Cardinals fans than anything else. In his next start, he beat the Cubs at Wrigley Field, battling through six innings with four earned runs. Then it was another home win, one unearned run over 8⅓ against the Pirates.

At age 29, Bob Tewksbury finally had some traction in the big leagues. He was starting regularly, eating up some innings, keeping the other guys off the scoreboard, and picking up wins. Tewksbury went into the second week of August with a 6–3 record, a 3.30 ERA and, most of all, a secure job.

"For once in my life, I don't feel like I'm worrying about going to Triple-A," he recalled. "I'm confident. I'm really happy. I'm in St. Louis. I love the city. I love the fans, the coaching staff. I'm really happy and it's showing in my performance."

It kept getting better from there. On August 12, he threw the second shutout of his career. Tewksbury breezed past a very good Pirates team—the eventual National League East champs—on six hits and 91 pitches. Only one Pirate even saw third base in the game, as Tewksbury cruised to his seventh win in 11 starts. His ERA dipped below 3.00 with the efficient showing.

Even that game, though, was a prelude for the game that Tewksbury remembers most clearly even now. Despite building a résumé that includes 110 wins, 277 starts, and an All-Star Game appearance, it's August 17, 1990 that stands out above any other day in Tewksbury's career. He flirted with a perfect game and threw a one-hit shutout, needing all of 79 pitches to put away the Astros at Busch Stadium. He struck out just three batters, but he didn't issue a walk and got 15 groundball outs. Houston was rendered helpless by an endless array of well-placed, well-planned pitches that might not have dented bread.

"I never felt like I owned anybody," he said. "My whole thing was pitch execution, and letting them put the ball in play. I threw strikes and that was always my m.o. I didn't feel like I had any better stuff that day, or any more dominance. I got them to put the ball in play, and they just never hit it on the sweet spot."

It was a steamy August night in St. Louis. The temperature was 91 degrees at game time in old Busch Stadium, and on the field it was even hotter, since they had yet to install natural grass at the circular ballpark. Tewksbury faced the Astros and another command-oriented righty, Bill Gullickson, on a Friday-night series opener matching two second-division teams. Grounders by Eric Yelding and Bill Doran and a flyball out to the shortstop by Ken Caminiti added up to a quick 1-2-3 top of the first.

The Cardinals manufactured a run in the bottom half of the inning in classic "Whiteyball" style, as Ozzie Smith walked, stole second, took third on a balk, and scored on a Willie McGee single. It was all the run support Tewksbury would need. He rolled through the second inning on three groundouts, sending down Franklin Stubbs, Glenn Wilson, and Tuffy Rhodes in order. Tewksbury put down a sacrifice in the bottom of the second that set up Coleman's two-run, two-out single, and St. Louis was in complete command of the game. It had already been an excellent day for Tewksbury, and now it was getting even better.

"My wife, Laura, flew in that day," he remembers. "We had gotten married in January of '89. So she went through it all with me, surgery and the whole rehab process, up and down in Louisville. She was working back home in New Hampshire, and she was coming out [to St. Louis]. I hadn't seen her in a long time, so I was really excited about that. I was confident from my last game. And she flew in that morning. So I wasn't thinking so much about the game as being with my wife. We went to lunch downtown and had a great time."

Rich Gedman and Rafael Ramirez flied out in the third, and Gullickson grounded out to shortstop for the ninth out. Tewksbury put down the top of the order in the fourth, with two more grounders before finally recording his first strikeout against Caminiti.

Twelve up, 12 down, and in the bottom half of the inning the Cardinals extended the lead to five runs. Gullickson was chased, and all the drama from the game was gone—except that Tewksbury still hadn't allowed a baserunner. With eight more pitches he dispensed with the middle of the Astros' order in the fifth. He'd thrown 42 pitches through five innings, never hitting so much as a mild speed bump.

"I found an aggressive team," he said. "I think I matched up well against their lineup. I pitched well against lefties. They had Caminiti, Gedman, Stubbs, they had a lineup of lefties. I don't think my command was any better than usual; I think it was solid. I hit my spots, I mixed up pitches."

When Gedman, Ramirez, and pinch hitter Dave Rohde went 1-2-3 on a fly ball, a 5-3 grounder, and a strikeout, Tewksbury started to realize what was going on. So did the fans—and especially Mrs. Tewksbury.

"Everything is just flowing," he said. "It's easy and everything feels good. And then it's not uncommon to go two or three innings, four innings, having a perfect game. And then I get to the fifth or sixth inning, and now it becomes like, 'Geez, there's something going on here.'

"After the game, my wife told me a story. Here it is hot and humid in St. Louis, and she bought this big lemonade in about the third inning. Now it's the sixth inning and I've got a perfect game going and she's got to go to the bathroom. But she doesn't want to get up to leave, and she doesn't."

The Cardinals went quickly in the bottom of the sixth, and Tewksbury worked a nine-pitch seventh. Yelding grounded out, Doran became the first and only victim of a swinging strikeout, and Caminiti flied out to right.

Then something unfortunate happened. Defying that classic baseball wisdom from the movie *Bull Durham*, Tewksbury started to think. Pitchers are at their best when they're concerned only with the pitch they are throwing at the moment. But Tewksbury couldn't help realizing what he was in the middle of.

"I get through the seventh inning, and I'm thinking, 'I've got a shot. I'm six outs away here.' And then I started thinking, 'What am I going to throw this guy leading off the inning?' No one is sitting next to me in the dugout. I'm really not talking to [catcher Todd] Zeile. I'm thinking, 'I know the significance of this.'"

He thought circles around himself, but finally he came to a conclusion. A groundball pitcher, Tewksbury decided to rely on his bread and butter. Throw a sinking fastball to Stubbs, get it down, get it on the edge of the plate, and get another grounder. Make things simple.

"Prior to that, the crowd was excited, but now they started to expect something," he said. "And so that's the only time I thought about it. I wasn't hyperventilating about, 'What am I going to throw this guy?' but I was to the point where it's like, 'Should I throw the curveball, should I throw the fastball?' And then I finally stopped the thinking. If my best pitch is a sinker, I'm going to throw him a fastball away."

Stubbs, a power hitter, might normally have gotten himself out on that fastball. Instead, he was patient. Stubbs kept back, stayed with the pitch, and poked a double to left field.

"I might have gotten it up a tad," Tewksbury admitted, "but he did a good job. If he tries to pull it, it's a groundball to second."

Tewksbury still thinks what if. But he also realizes that at the time, perhaps he wasn't prepared to handle that what if. Now employed by the Red Sox as a consultant in sports psychology, Tewksbury often thinks about how quickly the pressure built on him. He found that the atmosphere changed quickly, from no-stress to extremely charged. And he knew that from the seventh inning on, it was all only going to build.

"The anxiety is the thing you deal with," he said. "The pressure is going to continue to mount through the eighth inning and into the ninth inning. And I felt like if it did that, I was going to burst. What if it was two outs in the ninth? How do you deal with that?

"So on the one hand, when the hit happened, there's extreme relief. 'All right, now I can get back to pitching and get a shutout.' But there's also resounding disappointment in the fact that I didn't get it. So there's really an emotional spectrum that was unique, that I never experienced in any other game."

Mixed with the relief was a new and different sense of urgency. Although Tewksbury's no-hitter and perfect game were gone, he still had a shutout working—not to mention that the game still had to be won. Wilson, regularly a double-figure home run threat, was on deck and Tewksbury needed to get him out.

Often, when a pitcher works without baserunners for an extended period of time, it can be jarring to pitch with a man on. He's been pitching from the windup for so long that the switch to pitching from the stretch can be a problem. That first baserunner can quickly turn into multiple hits and runs.

"My high school baseball coach and my high school vice principal, they both played college ball and they were mentors to me," Tewksbury said. "And one of the things that they always told me was, if you give up a home run, you turn around, you get a ball from the umpire and you get the next guy out. And I took that approach after the hit. 'All right, I'm going to get the next guy out.' So some mental toughness came through in that."

He got ahead of Wilson in the count, 0-1, then induced a groundball to the left side of the infield from the veteran. That prevented Stubbs from reaching third base with one out, eliminating the possibility of the sacrifice fly.

"I thought, 'You know what, now I've got to get back to pitching,'" Tewksbury said. "I don't want him to advance to third base. I wanted a shutout. So I threw him a fastball in, and he hit a groundball to third or short. The runner didn't advance. I remember making that pitch, and I do remember that there was an acute awareness of not letting that deter my performance."

Rhodes flied out, and Stubbs advanced to third with two outs. Gedman grounded out to end the inning, and Tewksbury had escaped the only thing even resembling a jam that he faced all night. Perfection was gone, but Tewksbury was three outs away from the next best thing. A quick Cardinals turn at bat in the eighth meant Tewksbury was back out soon. Ramirez and pinch hitter Ken Oberkfell both grounded out to short, and Yelding flied out to end it.

Tewksbury had thrown a one-hit, no-walk, shutout. He'd done it with a Bob Gibson-like pace, finishing in one hour and 59 minutes. It wasn't exactly the way that Gibson did things, though.

"I've looked at the game tape, and I made some mistakes. They swung at some bad pitches. I didn't blow anybody away. They put the ball in play. One of the things about playing for those Cardinals teams was that you knew they were going to catch the ball. It makes it a lot easier to pitch when you know they're going to catch it."

Mostly, Tewksbury had shown the Cardinals, and the rest of baseball, that he was no "Quad-A" pitcher. He was a big leaguer, no matter what the radar gun said. He'd known it in his own mind since the game against Montreal. But after pitching against Houston, he made it clear to everyone else.

"The bigger picture for me, the full portrait of that year, is that I established myself as a major leaguer," he said. "Whether it was a perfect game or a one-hitter, my ultimate goal was to be in the big leagues and to have a long career. And I think that game gave me some clout that I belonged."

Ironically, Tewksbury actually slumped after his one-hitter. He turned in two more excellent games in his next two starts, but went 1-5 in September with a 6.68 ERA. But that was just the kind of slide that his previous two months allowed him. Tewksbury was a major leaguer, and finally he had a little bit of a cushion. It took him until he was 29 to get it, but that just made his arrival sweeter.

"With the struggles that I had, certainly it enhanced my appreciation for what it meant to finally reach the pinnacle," he said. "And ultimately, I played another eight years after that. I gained appreciation for all that. I think sometimes, the young players who get rushed to the big leagues for whatever reason . . . they kind of take things for granted."

Tewksbury made 30 starts for the Cardinals in 1991, posting 11 wins and a 3.25 ERA. In 1992, he enjoyed a career year. Just three years after spending most of the season in the minors, Tewksbury went 16-5 in '92. He walked a stunning 20 batters in 233 innings, finished second in the league with a 2.16 ERA, and placed third in the Cy Young balloting. He won 17 more for the Cardinals in 1993, and pitched until he was 37. Tewksbury still ranks among the all-time leaders in fewest walks per nine innings pitched. And he lasted long enough to make some money in the game, playing in the seven-figure era after starting out when the major league minimum was $68,000.

Just as Tewksbury's career path was atypical, so has his post-playing life been. After he retired, Tewksbury wrapped up his undergraduate degree in physical education and began working as a consultant with the Red Sox. From there, an amateur interest in sports psychology drew him to pursue a graduate degree in the field. Now he works with Red Sox minor leaguers on mastering the mental side of the game. And he realizes that if he'd done a better job of that on August 17, 1990, he might have a perfect game to his credit.

Or he might not.

"Now that I've been in the field and I'm doing the work that I'm doing with players, I look back at that moment," he said. "And I think, 'I threw the pitch I wanted to throw, I can live with that.' But was there anything I could have done? Was it the fear of dealing with the pressure in the ninth inning that somehow took away from executing the pitch more perfectly? I don't know."

It's not something that keeps him up at night. It wasn't even something that kept him up at night back in 1990. But sometimes, at the strangest moments, Tewksbury thinks about what almost happened for him.

"I remember coming home after the season," he said. "My wife and I had just bought a house. It was mid-October or something, I was raking leaves, and it kind of hit me. I was six outs away from a perfect game. And then I was kind of running through it, like, 'Gollee! Should I have thrown him another pitch?' And I started to replay this thing months later. But at the time, I slept like a baby that night. I was totally content."

CHAPTER 12

JASON ISRINGHAUSEN

The game of Jason Isringhausen's life should have come on October 27, 2006. He should have followed in the footsteps of a player he cheered when he was a kid. Ever since Isringhausen signed with the Cardinals in the winter of 2001–2002, he wanted to replicate Bruce Sutter. He wanted to be the man on the mound when St. Louis closed out a world championship.

Isringhausen is a native of the St. Louis area and a lifetime Cardinals fan. He grew up on the Illinois side of the Mississippi River, following the team that he later got to pitch for. Just like everyone else in the region, he had last celebrated a Redbirds World Series title in 1982—when he was 10. He came close more than once. In 2002 the Cards were favorites to win the pennant, but they were eliminated in the National League Championship Series. In 2004 he experienced the next best thing, when he got the last out of the NLCS for the Cards' first pennant in 17 years.

When his team completed its return to glory in '06, though, Isringhausen was in the same position as he had been in '82. He was a spectator, a fan, unable to contribute. He was a fan with great access, that's for sure. He got his champagne shower along with his teammates after they dusted off the Tigers in five games. He rode in the parade in downtown St. Louis. He got a World Series ring. But it just wasn't quite right. Isringhausen had helped put the Cardinals in position to win it all. He was their closer for the first five months of the season, finishing games while they amassed a seemingly insurmountable lead in the National League Central.

But he hadn't delivered in the end, because he was recuperating from a serious hip operation. The Cardinals closer was physically unable to finish the job, and it ate at him—even as he was delighted for his friends, his teammates, and his protégé. To Isringhausen's credit, he's about the only person in the Cardinals organization who sells his own contributions so short. Playing in absolute agony, Isringhausen gutted out five months of a season when every single pitch shot pain through his body. If his teammates didn't know at the time, they learned later.

He was charged with a galling 10 blown saves thanks to a terrible loss of command, but he also successfully converted 33 chances. And even after he went under the knife, he helped. Some would say that's when he helped most of all. Isringhausen was already a father figure—or at least a big brother figure—in the young Cardinals bullpen. After he went down to injury, he helped shepherd his replacement, Adam Wainwright, through the postseason en route to the title. Wainwright got the final out of all three series, but everyone knew it was supposed to be Isringhausen. Wainwright himself knew it.

Yet "Izzy" gave of himself fully. He helped Wainwright out with tips and hints. He never complained. He did what he could to keep the bullpen loose. He was agonizing, but he always put the team before himself. Isringhausen was as engaged as an injured player can be.

"Watching the final outs of all the series, it's no fun to watch," Isringhausen says. "If [Wainwright] was a bad guy I probably wouldn't like him. But he's too nice to not like. Myself and [Mark] Mulder, we were the two broken guys. We stayed out of the way a little bit. But I still got a ring, and that's more than a lot of people have. It still hurts a little bit, because that was supposed to be me."

Even before his miserable 2006, Isringhausen was a polarizing player among Cardinals fans. Isringhausen at his very best is something of a fasten-your-seatbelts closer, a guy who often allows some baserunners before getting the job done. Closing, you might say, is

A hometown Cardinals fan, it killed Jason Isringhausen not to be able to pitch in the World Series. Making it back to pitch the next year was a victory in itself.
AP/WWP

more of an art than a science for him.

He's also lost some zip on his fastball thanks to a series of surgeries and the simple march of age. So he's become a different kind of pitcher in the later years of his career. Once a classic power pitcher, featuring high-90s gas and a neck-breaking curveball, Isringhausen made the transition to rely more on locating a cut fastball. Thus, a bad day can be a really bad day these days. When you make a mistake with an 89-mph cutter, it's much more likely to leave the park than a mistake on a 96-mph heater.

So when Isringhausen started the '06 season shakily, it didn't sit well with the faithful. Calls for his removal from the ninth inning, or even trading or releasing the franchise's all-time saves leader, grew louder and louder as the season went on.

He got the save on Opening Day despite walking two Phillies. On April 9 in Chicago, he took the loss when he permitted two more walks followed by a home run in a tie game. Isringhausen's ERA didn't get under 5.00 until May 9, but around that time he started to get it together. His hip caused him tremendous pain every time he landed on the mound, but he was surviving.

"As a reliever, you have to know there's a difference between hurt and sore," he says. "I was hurting, but in the same sense, I could still get people out. Just not on as consistent a basis as usual. So for a long time I went out there and kind of winged it and tried to make up stuff and get people out whatever way I could. I gave up a lot of home runs because of backup cutters, because I couldn't finish that pitch."

His season started turning again for the worse in June. A pitcher who went all of 2002 without allowing a home run served up seven in 30⅔ innings from early June to late October. He was getting booed at home, by fans who pride themselves on being the best in baseball. Isringhausen simply couldn't land with any stability when he delivered the ball. He pushed off of his back leg with no problem. His arm was strong. But his front leg, his landing leg, couldn't withstand the force of his 230 pounds coming down on it.

"My leg would collapse, and then my whole upper body would collapse, and it would just leave my arm out there hanging," he explained the following spring. "So you're actually letting go of it too soon. I couldn't finish my pitches. That's why a lot of cutters were staying in the middle of the plate. And then I lose my velocity when

I throw like that. If a right-hander is leaning out over the plate and it comes right down the middle, then it's not good."

Occasionally, he would drop a hint to reporters that something wasn't right, but he never came right out and said it. So fans had no idea what he was dealing with. He's not entirely sure that manager Tony La Russa and the rest of the staff even realized.

"I don't think so," he says. "I didn't really tell anybody. I don't make excuses. I'm not like other people that are always having an excuse for why they're doing bad. I think the trainers knew. I'm sure they knew, but we never talked about it. We never addressed it."

The struggles came to a head in early September in Washington. Isringhausen took his 10th blown save in a particularly crushing game for the Cardinals. They had rallied from a 5-3 deficit to score three runs in the final three innings, handing their closer a 6-5 lead in the ninth. Isringhausen was all but helpless to protect the advantage, though. Two walks and a hit batter loaded the bases, and Jose Vidro singled in two runs to end the game.

Until that game, Isringhausen had resisted the notion of stepping aside. He could tolerate the pain enough to do his job, and he believed he was needed. He was doing what he felt was best for the Cardinals, even if it was taking a huge toll on both his body and his pride.

"Who was going to take my place? I wasn't thinking about myself," he says. "I was thinking about my team. That's the way I have to do it. When I quit, we had a nine-game lead and a month to go. I thought we were pretty good to go. But it just got to the point where I had had enough."

He hinted to reporters after the game in Washington that he might need some down time, and the following day in Arizona he made it official. He notified the club that he was no longer able to do his job. It wasn't a matter of discomfort; it was simply that the ineffectiveness became too much to bear.

"I thought I wasn't doing the team any good," he says. "We had a nine-game lead, and I just didn't think I could close games effectively the way we needed for that last month. With a nine-game lead, I thought we could patch it together and figure it out. But we got into the playoffs and the rest is history. It didn't get worse pain-wise. There wasn't anything else I could do to it. It was already screwed up. I just couldn't get people out effectively and I was killing the team. It's a big letdown when you battle your ass off for eight innings and I come in and blow it on a home run."

In the first days after Isringhausen was sidelined, he and the team explored nonsurgical options. He received a cortisone shot to ease the pain, but there was little real hope for avoiding an operation. A throwing session after the shot revealed the same difficulties he'd had before. He needed hip surgery. Isringhausen's condition dated back to mid-2004, when he first began feeling some discomfort. Over the ensuing winter, he had a relatively minor procedure, repairing some damage to the joint's labrum. This operation would be more serious. The earlier surgery had been done by team Dr. George Paletta, but this time around he would visit a hip specialist.

The question was just how invasive the operation would be. Until the surgeon actually began the procedure, there was no being sure just how extensive his task was. The possibilities ranged from Isringhausen returning more or less at the start of 2008 to the pitcher being finished pitching for good. He literally wouldn't know until he came out of anesthesia whether he would be able to continue pitching.

"Any time they open you up, you really have no idea what's going to happen or how it's going to come out," he says, but that was especially true with Isringhausen's hip operation. "Going into the surgery, I didn't know when I woke up what it was going to be. If they had to resurface the joint, I probably would never pitch again."

Following the operation by Dr. J. Thomas Byrd in Nashville, Isringhausen awoke in a hospital bed. He looked to his wife for the news, good or bad. It was good. Isringhausen needed debridement, or a clean-up, of arthritis in his hip as well as work to ease an impingement in the joint. The second procedure was the more involved. Byrd performed a "mild re-contouring" of the femoral head of the joint. The femoral head is essentially the ball in the ball-and-socket joint of the hip.

"The first thing I did was look at Lorrie and I was like, 'What did they do?' and she told me, and I was like, 'OK good.' I was excited. And it was time to get to work."

As far as Isringhausen was concerned, rehab started as soon as he was able to get out of bed. It would be a long and difficult process, and to some extent, he was a test case. The operation he had undergone was not typical for baseball players. It was more commonly a football operation, explaining why he had the Tennessee Titans team doctor do the surgery.

"They said there's never been a pitcher that's had it and came back to be effective," he says. "So yeah, I had doubt in my mind. But there's a first for everything, I figured. I was somewhat of a guinea pig."

So Isringhausen spent the winter rehabilitating. That in itself was not unusual. His litany of injuries is staggering. Isringhausen has undergone multiple surgical procedures on his elbow, shoulder, and hip. So it's stranger for him to have a winter where he's not coming back from something. When Isringhausen reported to Spring Training, he was one of the biggest stories in Jupiter, Florida. Every time he did anything, it drew attention. His first throwing session off a mound was treated like a playoff game.

"You've got a lot of people watching, and you're kind of singled out," he says. "Every pitch, when you land on it, you're kind of wondering how it's going to feel. It feels a little tweaky, but then as you get going, it gets better and better. That first day out there was kind of nerve-wracking because you've got all the coaches, you've got the general manager, all the press, and the cameras. And it's like, 'What am I going to do if I go out there and I fall down?'"

He didn't fall down, but the Cardinals proceeded slowly. Isringhausen wasn't rushed. He didn't appear in a game until the second half of Grapefruit League play, building gradually and steadily. Remarkably, everything went well. A tricky joint and a tricky surgery held up beautifully under the Florida sun. As camp went on, Isringhausen's status went from one of the team's bigger questions to one of its better stories.

He knew, though, that nothing is really certain until the lights are on. Success in the Grapefruit League doesn't necessarily translate to success in the National League. And even in an exhibition game, you can't fully replicate the level of exertion and intensity that's found in a regular-season contest.

"It's totally different," he says. "Half the time [in Spring Training] they're not even swinging the bat. They're just kind of watching pitches and checking things out. There's always doubt about when the bell rings and you have to pitch for six months no matter what."

Ideally, Isringhausen would have returned triumphantly. He would have notched a save on Opening Night against the Mets, the team Wainwright closed out in the National League Championship Series a year earlier. Ace Chris Carpenter would have gone eight innings before handing over to his friend and teammate, and Isringhausen would have brought the win home.

Very little worked out ideally for the Cardinals in 2007, though. On Opening Night, Carpenter was knocked around, allowing five runs in six innings. The season's second game was close, but still didn't bring a save chance. In game No. 3, La Russa finally turned to his closer, but it was mop-up work.

Regardless, it was the most enjoyable 10-0 deficit Isringhausen ever pitched with. Braden Looper, who moved to the rotation in part because of Isringhausen's return to health, pitched adequately. Looper allowed three runs over six innings, a quality start. But in the middle innings, the St. Louis bullpen sputtered. Josh Hancock was charged with two runs, and Russ Springer with five.

Isringhausen needed to get in a game, so he finished off the procession of relievers. And it was delightfully uneventful. David Wright led off the inning. Wright fouled off a pitch up in the strike zone, then flied out to center field for the first out. There was no tentativeness for Isringhausen once he was on the mound. If he wondered before he took the field, he thought only about doing his job once he had the ball in his hand.

"I'm the type of guy that, whenever I've had surgery, if they fixed it, they fixed it," he says. "So when they tell me it's time to go, they give me the OK to go, I go as hard as I can. And I've always done that. So that never entered my mind at all about taking it easy."

The second hitter was outfielder Lastings Milledge. Isringhausen got ahead, 0-1, then threw three straight balls to the youngster. But he fought back with a called strike, and got Milledge to ground out to third base. Two up, two down. Then he finished things off quickly. Shawn Green took a ball, then made it back-to-back outs on the ground. Isringhausen had proven to himself that his body could hold up to pitching in the Major Leagues once again.

"It's one of those deals where you have a beer and look back on it and have a big smile," he says. "I was proud of myself a little bit. Plus the first game back was against the Mets, my old team. It was gratifying all the way around. I just wanted to let myself know I was back."

Two days later, he notched his first save, against the Astros at cozy Minute Maid Park. He gave up a run in the process, but he was 1 for 1. Early the next week in Pittsburgh, he went back-to-back games for the first time. Soon the milestones became matters of routine.

"That first game back, and then getting the first save, it's just a big weight lifted off your shoulders," he says. "As I went along in Spring Training, there were little pains here and there. So I didn't know how the whole season was going to come about. But the whole season was great."

Perhaps as sweet as anything was the reception from the home fans. When the stories came out about what Isringhausen had battled the previous year, fan opinion started to shift. When he got off to a hot start, that sentiment was further solidified.

"If I'd pitched bad, they would have given me the same treatment no matter what," he says stoically. "Doing what I do, you either get booed or you get cheered. There's no in between."

The cheers stuck around for the remainder of the year. Buoyed by a strong start, Isringhausen enjoyed a bounce-back season. A year after taking 10 blown saves and eight losses, he was charged with two blown saves and no defeats in 2007. He cut his home runs by more than half, and slashed his walk rate. Isringhausen wasn't done in 2006. He was just hurt. Once he was healthy again, he was effective again. He was the same pitcher he'd been all those years, and if he took fans on more of a ride than they liked sometimes, they were satisfied with the end result more often than not.

The recovery even contributed to an extra year for Isringhausen with his home team. The Cardinals held a contract option on him for 2008, and that option looked to be in severe jeopardy following '06. After his '07 comeback, picking up the extra year was a simple choice. Isringhausen was rewarded with at least one more year pitching for his favorite club, and at least one more chance to be the guy with his arms in the air at the end of October.

CHAPTER 13

JOSE OQUENDO

Jose Oquendo really can do it all, and not just on the baseball field. Oquendo, beloved by fans as the "Secret Weapon" of the St. Louis teams of the late 1980s and early 1990s, has long been an athletic Renaissance man.

As a youngster in Puerto Rico, Oquendo recalls spending game after game as a catcher. A little later in his teen years, he pitched. It wasn't until shortly before Oquendo left the island to play pro ball on the U.S. mainland that he became primarily an infielder.

As a coach for the current-day Cards, Oquendo is a chatterbox in English and Spanish, depending on who is closest to his steady stream of gab. He mans the third-base box, directing traffic on the bases, and he also has established himself as one of the best coaches of infield technique in the game. Oquendo has yet to manage in the major leagues, but he helmed the Puerto Rican team in the World Baseball Classic, and few jobs in baseball require more all-around skill than managing a team. Especially when that team consists of stars from all over baseball. And though you'd get some argument from a teammate or two, Oquendo is probably also the best golfer to wear the "birds on the bat" in quite a long time.

So it's just part and parcel that in 1988, Oquendo did everything you can do on a baseball field. What's remarkable is that Oquendo did it all well. He even acquitted himself ably on the pitcher's mound, twirling four innings in what remains his most memorable day on the ball field.

By the time the '88 season had ended, Oquendo had played every position on the field, not so much as a gimmick but because in most cases, he was needed. Whereas Scott Sheldon bounced around in the space of five innings of a September 2000 contest, Oquendo played all over the field over the span of a season. He didn't do it all in one game, and in fact bristles at that misconception. He did it in the normal course of a season.

"I enjoyed the way it happened," he says. "A lot of times guys say, 'Did you play all nine just to do it?' I say, 'No, I played all nine because they needed me to do it.' It was a need more than just throwing me out there to see if I could play all nine. We got in situations where I had to play all nine positions."

Oquendo's catching appearance, on September 24, 1988, is the only part of his defensive cycle that could be called anything like a stunt. He caught for an inning in a blowout while the Redbirds still had a catcher available. Other than that, manager Whitey Herzog used Oquendo only when and where he thought the utility man could help his ballclub. Herzog was creative and aggressive as a skipper—but he was neither crazy nor stupid.

By April 11 of '88, Oquendo had played in six games at three different positions—third base, right field, and shortstop. Within four more weeks he'd made his season debuts at first and second base, and on May 13 he got the call in center field for Herzog's 'Birds.

"I'd rather be in the game than sitting on the bench doing nothing," Oquendo says. "I didn't care where I wanted to play. I just wanted to be in there."

The season wasn't even six weeks old, and the Secret Weapon had already been deployed everywhere but left field, behind the plate, and on the mound. Little did Oquendo know that he'd scratch off one more position the next night. The woeful Braves, still three years away from the beginning of their reign atop the National League, faced the defending league champion Cardinals at Busch Stadium on a Saturday night. Atlanta started Zane Smith, the closest thing it had to an ace, against rookie wunderkind Chris Carpenter.

Known as the "Secret Weapon," Jose Oquendo is as loved by St. Louis fans today as a coach as he was during his playing days. *Brace Photos*

Oquendo, as had typically been the case so far that season, was not in the starting lineup. Equally typically, he played a vital role in how the game unfolded. The Cardinals took a quick 3-0 lead behind RBI singles from Terry Pendleton and Vince Coleman and a bases-loaded walk to Tom Brunansky. Atlanta rallied for four in the fourth to pull ahead, with a walk, a single, a double, a triple, and a sacrifice fly. However, the Bravos gave back two runs in the bottom half of the frame, and St. Louis was on top again. Willie McGee rapped an RBI single and Pendleton drove in another run with a double. The score remained 5-4 until Andres Thomas' RBI groundout tied it in the seventh.

That run came with Scott Terry on the mound, the third Cardinals pitcher of the day. Carpenter had lasted six innings, with Steve Peters getting a single out before Terry entered. Ken Dayley tossed the eighth, and Herzog summoned closer Todd Worrell in the tie game in the ninth. In the lineup maneuvering that got Worrell on the field, Oquendo also entered.

He took over as the first baseman, batting—appropriately, it would later turn out—in the ninth spot. Worrell went into the No. 6 hole, which had been occupied by first baseman Bob Horner. Worrell twirled three outstanding innings, allowing a hit, a walk, and no runs. But that was all the career reliever could handle, and he was removed after equaling a career high in innings. After Worrell gave way to a pinch hitter, Herzog turned to Bob Forsch, a starter by trade.

And on it dragged. Forsch, like Worrell, breezed through three innings until his spot came up in the batting order. Pinch hitter Duane Walker singled to lead off the 14th, and Oquendo—in the middle of it as usual—bunted him over to second. But the Cards couldn't get the run home, and it was on to the 15th. This was not a game for the out of shape, that much is certain. By the time it was over, Atlanta and St. Louis had played for five hours and 40 minutes.

"We had a few games like that," Oquendo says. "We don't think about it. One year I think I played 163 games. It's just one game. We don't think about that stuff. We just keep going. That's the way we grew up, having fun."

Journeyman Randy O'Neal pitched a single inning, but he wasn't the man Herzog had in mind as his long reliever. For the 16th inning, O'Neal left the game. Oquendo, who had pitched one inning in a blowout game the previous August, took the mound. Walker moved from left field to first base, and Jose DeLeon, the next day's starting pitcher, came in to play left.

"I don't think [Herzog] thought that I could pitch," Oquendo admits. "But I was kind of durable, a guy who liked playing different positions, and we ran out of pitchers. I was the guy to waste, to use in that situation. *[laughs]* We didn't have any choice but to do that.

"He knew that I would do anything that needed to be done. I was already playing all the other positions in the field and he knew I had a good arm at that time and I was durable. I wasn't a guy who got hurt a lot. So it was an ideal situation."

Well, maybe not ideal. But it could have been worse. Oquendo even had an out pitch, such as it was, as part of a surprisingly broad repertoire.

"I had a lot of junk," he recalls. "I threw a lot of split-fingers, fastballs, and little sliders that didn't break. But the main pitch was the split-finger. I usually messed around with guys when we played catch, and I threw [the splitter] a lot playing catch. It was easy for me to grip it that way and throw it over. It was a good pitch."

Oquendo was greeted by the middle of the Braves' order. And he was greeted rudely. Left fielder Ken Griffey Sr., a left-handed hitter, roped a double to open the inning. Oquendo issued an intentional walk to another lefty swinger, Gerald Perry, bringing up Ozzie Virgil. The catcher, a right-handed hitter, did the Cardinals a little bit of a favor when he singled to the opposite field. Had he pulled the ball, it would have been up to DeLeon to make the play, but instead Brunansky threw out Griffey trying to score.

Oquendo's odyssey had almost ended before it really got going, but Brunansky bailed him out. Another lefty, Ken Oberkfell, flied out, bringing up dangerous righty rookie Ron Gant. That's when Herzog unveiled the last piece of his late-innings strategy. Brunansky and DeLeon switched fields, with Brunansky taking over where Gant was more likely to hit the ball. They would alternate a boggling 10 more times over the final four innings as Herzog attempted to maximize his team's defensive prowess. For the most part, it was Brunansky in right field for a left-handed hitter, and in left field for a right-hander.

"It wasn't distracting," Oquendo insists. "Whitey did some stuff before, so we knew that in certain situations he would sometimes put Worrell in the outfield [and things like that]."

Gant got hold of a ball, but fortunately he hit it to center, where three-time Gold Glover McGee was patrolling the turf. Oquendo and the Cardinals were out of the inning, and the two clubs were headed to the bottom of the 16th.

It was a quick frame, with Luis Alicea, Walker, and Oquendo going 1-2-3 on grounders, and Oquendo headed back to the mound. This time he retired the leadoff man, which happened to be opposing pitcher Rick Mahler. Dion James singled, and another Brunansky-DeLeon flip put the right fielder back in left field and the pitcher in right. This time, DeLeon was tested, but he corralled Andres Thomas' fly ball. Dale Murphy, a two-time MVP, grounded out to end the inning. Two innings in, Oquendo was sailing.

"Everybody was laughing," Oquendo remembers. "Every time I got out of big trouble that I got into, they gave me high-fives in the dugout. We had fun. It was fun from both sides. I think both teams laughed. We wanted to beat each other, but it was fun."

The problem was, he wasn't getting any help. His teammates again went quickly and harmlessly in the 17th, as DeLeon, Ozzie Smith, and McGee were retired in order. So it fell to Oquendo to keep the tie in effect and give his team the chance to win.

He got off to his best start yet in the 18th. With Brunansky back in right field, Griffey flied out to center and Perry flied out to Brunansky. But Oquendo began to have trouble with his control, issuing consecutive walks to Virgil and Oberkfell. The winning run had reached scoring position, but Herzog's "fireman" remained unrattled.

"I got in a lot of trouble," Oquendo acknowledges. "I walked a lot of guys. It would be a big situation, and most of the time, I wouldn't say the right guy came up to the plate, but I'd have a guy that was a free swinger. I'd throw a lot of split-fingers, and [get out of it]."

Mahler, pitching his seventh inning of relief, finally found himself in a jam in the 18th. Brunansky led off the inning with a single and took second on an error. Tom Lawless attempted a sacrifice, but reached on an error, and the Cardinals had men on the corners with no outs. A groundball advanced Lawless, and Alicea walked to load the bases.

Oquendo understandably allowed his mind to wander a little bit—he realized he could be the winning pitcher. It had been 20 years, since Rocky Colavito pitched for the Yankees in 1968, that a non-pitcher had been credited with the victory in a major league game. Oquendo nearly ended that streak.

"I said, 'Hey, I'm going to have a chance here.' They walked to load the bases, and I said, 'Man, I can win this game with a sacrifice or a groundball or whatever.' And the guy hit a line-drive double play, and I was mad at him. But that's part of the game."

Walker did in fact hit into a 6-5 double play. Oquendo went from pondering his place in history to pitching a fourth inning. He fanned Mahler, his only strikeout, but walked James. Thomas popped up, and he walked Murphy. Given yet another shot at the infielder, Griffey finally took advantage with a two-run double. Perry was walked intentionally before Virgil grounded out to end the inning.

The Cardinals couldn't rally in the bottom of the 19th, and a long, hot, bizarre night ended with Oquendo as the losing pitcher. His line was respectable—two runs in four innings—despite the six walks. And he surely had a story to tell, and a legion of new fans.

"I think everybody stayed," he says. "Everybody waited until the end of the game. A few guys who were walking out and came back into the game when I came in to pitch. It was fun. People enjoy it. I still have a lot of guys talking about that day. Some guys come up to me and say, 'Hey, I was at that game that you pitched.'"

Oquendo's pitching career didn't end in '88. He made one more appearance on the mound three years later, again versus the Braves. The circumstances the second time around, however, changed drastically. Oquendo entered a game the Cardinals trailed, 14-1, in the eighth inning. His control was again an issue, as he walked two batters and permitted three runs. Oquendo finished his major league pitching career with three appearances, six innings pitched and a 12.00 ERA. He did record a second strikeout, however, and it was bigger game than Mahler. In the '91 game, Oquendo caught Deion Sanders looking for career strikeout No. 2.

Despite Oquendo's lengthy career and successful life in baseball, for many of the people he encounters, pitching is the first thing that comes to mind. That's especially true for his opponents from those halcyon days as a hurler.

"I've run into Chuck Tanner, the manager of Atlanta, and we have fun about it," Oquendo says. "I also run into a couple of the players, like Deion Sanders, and Ken Griffey when we go to Cincinnati. We have fun and we laugh about it. I was good friends with Mahler, who pitched in that game. When we play golf, we joke about it."

Even the players he coaches now bring it up—sometimes because they want a pointer or two. During the 2007 season, St. Louis called on two different position players to pitch on a total of three occasions: Scott Spiezio once and Aaron Miles twice. Each of the do-it-all utility men has a little Oquendo in him, with a willingness to do whatever, whenever. So naturally, they sought out Oquendo for tips when they found out they were pitching. He had simple advice: slower is better. Keep it below the hitting speed and you'll be just fine. Try to be a pitcher, and you'll just get hit.

"We joke a little bit," he says. "We say keep the ball below the radar gun. Don't throw too hard. If anything, throw less to throw off some of the hitters. Because if you try to throw hard, you're going to throw BP probably. So throw below that.

"Guys come up to me, 'When you pitched, how did you do it? What did you do?' Well, I tried to throw as slow as I could."

Oquendo remembers the four-inning appearance vividly 20 years later. He could hardly forget, as often as it's brought up. But 24 hours later, he had a reminder of a different kind. His right arm was absolutely killing him, and he couldn't take a day to rest it. McGee was unavailable due to injury, so a day after DeLeon played left and right, Oquendo played center.

"We do what we've got to do as players," he says. "We tried not to complain about how tired we are or how sore we get in the game. We just try to go as long as we can and hopefully come out on top. I couldn't even raise [my arm]. But Willie got hurt and Whitey put me in center field. I was throwing the ball almost underhand because I couldn't get my arm back up. But it was sore for a few days, and then I took a couple Advil and I was good to go."

Whether by coincidence or as a reward, Oquendo soon found himself in the lineup regularly after his pitching appearance. He started five of the season's first 35 games. Over St. Louis' next 68 contests, Oquendo was in the starting nine 64 times. He enjoyed a fine year, putting up a .350 on-base percentage and playing 148 games on the season.

The next year, Oquendo played every single game and put up a .375 OBP. It's not overstating things to say that the night Oquendo pitched was his last night as a bench player. The causation may not be quite so clear, but the coincidence is striking.

Oquendo became something of a cult figure for his versatility and his personality, but it sells him short to view him as a novelty. He was a quality ballplayer, posting very good OBPs in just about every season that he played regularly. He was willing to take a walk and hard to strike out. And there's a reason he kept getting plugged in at so many different positions—he was a good defender.

His career even inspired Hall of Fame dreams of a sort. In 2004, Major League Baseball Productions helped present a mock documentary about Oquendo. Two fans embarked on a "quest" to secure enshrinement for Oquendo in Cooperstown. They obviously fell short, but the program illustrates the affection for Oquendo in St. Louis.

Now he makes his money in the coach's box, and he'd love to land a managerial job. After playing under Herzog, he coaches under Tony La Russa, meaning he's learned from two legitimate Hall of Fame candidates. La Russa insists that Oquendo will make an excellent manager when he gets the chance. Oquendo knows that's partly from having good teachers. He also believes that the way he played the game led to his ability to be a successful coach.

"Even then, I wasn't a big baserunner, but I understood the importance of running," he explains. "Being aware, being prepared, anticipating, stuff like that helped me out a lot. I take coaching like I'm a scared guy out there. I don't want to screw up. So I need to be in the game from the first inning to the end of the game. I get worn out mentally thinking about what I'm going to do, how we can score this guy from first."

He says it's every bit as stressful as playing was, though perhaps not quite as physically draining—especially on those steamy St. Louis nights. Fortunately, the turf is gone, and new Busch Stadium isn't quite as hot as the previous park was.

One thing definitely hasn't changed—you can't keep Oquendo quiet.

"I'm out there talking to hitters," he says. "Some of the guys don't like me to say anything when they hit, but I can't help it. I'm trying to help them out. When they're on the bases, they always tell me to shut up, because I talk too much and make them nervous. I say, 'If you're nervous, that means you're prepared.'"

The effort, the preparation, and the sunny disposition all made Oquendo a popular teammate. His ability, meanwhile, made him a fine baseball player. The combination means that he remains a favorite in St. Louis more than a decade after he stopped playing. He returns the love. It's a perfect match of fan favorite and adoring city, not to mention capable coach with quality ballclub.

"The fans in St. Louis, they're big supporters of the players," Oquendo says. "Even the ones who were here for a few days, or a few years, when they come back, the fans still remember those guys. And I was fortunate to be in St. Louis for 10 years, and we had some wins.

"It's a privilege [to be a fan favorite]. It's a big honor to be part of an organization that has a big tradition. I think fans appreciate that and they know how much respect and tradition the Cardinals have."

CHAPTER 14

RICK HORTON

When the Padres left old Qualcomm Stadium—better known as Jack Murphy Stadium, or more affectionately, "The Murph"—they told a story about Cardinals pitcher Rick Horton. Actually, Horton went by a more casual name back in his playing days too; he was Ricky, not Rick. And if you're being picky, when they tell the story in San Diego, they're not really talking about Horton. Whether it's Rick or Ricky, in the San Diego version he's overshadowed by someone known simply as "The Chicken." Oh, and also a horse.

June 29, 1984 was an odd and memorable day at the ballpark. That much is for sure.

Horton, then a rookie making his fourth major league start, enjoyed the best game of his career that day. He had no idea at the time that one of the most famous incidents at the old stadium took place behind him at the same time. He also had no idea, truth be told, that he'd never pitch another game like that.

A well-spoken and likeable University of Virginia product, Horton was drafted by the Cardinals in the fourth round in 1980. He climbed the ladder through the St. Louis system, and put himself in position to make the club in the spring of 1984.

"I had pitched in winter ball for Hal Lanier, who was our third-base coach," Horton recalls. "Hal came to me the last day of Spring Training and said, 'If you pitch well this last day of Spring Training you'll make the team, and if you don't, you won't. I thought you'd want to know that.'"

Horton got the job done in that Grapefruit League contest, and he squeezed his way onto the staff as a reliever. He was primarily a mop-up man in the early going, but by June he'd gained a chance to make a few starts. The rookie took a sensational 1.73 ERA into the game in San Diego, and that was just one reason he had a smile on his face when he was getting ready for start No. 4.

"San Diego is a great place to pitch anyway," Horton says. "They had a high mound. I loved the weather there. They had a lot of lefties in their lineup. I just loved pitching in San Diego. I had relatives there, a cousin who came to the game that night, and my wife happened to be there too. And I just had one of those days where you're just absolutely in the zone."

He threw a fastball, a slider, and a changeup, relying on the change as an out pitch. Horton was rarely dominant, but he usually kept the ball in the park and he could pitch in a variety of roles and situations. He stayed around the major leagues for seven seasons, retiring after a second tour with the Cardinals. Horton also pitched for the White Sox and Dodgers.

In his post-playing life, he's still around the Cardinals. Horton works with the Fellowship of Christian Athletes in St. Louis, and he calls Cardinals games on TV and occasionally radio. He was a role player when he pitched, arguably a more prominent presence in St. Louis 20 years after his career ended.

Horton came into the San Diego game on a roll that dated back several months. After making the team in Spring Training he had pitched exceptionally well as a reliever, finally getting a shot to start for the Cards. In each of Horton's three starts he'd pitched at least respectably, and he'd won two of them. He had yet to allow more than two earned runs in a start despite facing quality competition each time. He even found himself in line for a little extra cash, and that's never a bad thing, especially as a rookie.

"What I really remember thinking is that I wanted to establish myself as a starting pitcher," Horton says. "I went to see the general manager after I made the team. I told him I thought I could be a

---

Rick Horton had no idea at the time that he was experiencing the greatest individual highlight of his career early in his rookie season. *Brace Photos*

starter. And he said, 'Well, we're not really ready for that, but if you're a starter, I'll give you $10,000 more than the minimum.'

"That wasn't contractual. It was just a conversation with Joe McDonald. He said it, I heard it, I remembered it, but I never thought of it again until he called me in his office and said, 'I told you I'd give you more money,' and he gave it to me. So I made more money than the minimum as a rookie based on establishing myself as a starting pitcher around that time."

So Horton entered his game at San Diego with confidence, and perhaps a little naïveté about what was possible and what could be expected in the major leagues. Not that that's a bad state of mind to be in. Facing a team that ultimately won the National League pennant, Horton took command quickly and never let the Padres get anything going. He retired Alan Wiggins, Tony Gwynn, and Steve Garvey in order after St. Louis had a three-up, three-down top of the first.

The Cardinals collected two hits but not a run in the second, and Horton again twirled a perfect inning in the bottom half, this time against Carmelo Martinez, Terry Kennedy, and Kevin McReynolds. Horton's own sacrifice put Ozzie Smith in position to score on Lonnie Smith's third-inning single, and the Cardinals led, 1-0. The bottom third of the order, Greg Nettles, Garry Templeton, and pitcher Eric Show, put up little fight in the third, and Horton had accomplished his first goal of the afternoon.

"It's three three-inning games," Horton explains. "Everything I could do, I was going to focus on throwing three-inning games. Trying to beat the other guy in three-inning games. It's me against him.

"So the fourth inning comes, OK, first game's over. I won, I lost, whatever. It's the fourth inning, and all I'm thinking about is, my competition right now is to win this three-inning game. My thought was, if I think too much about what I did or what I have to do, I'm in trouble. So it helped me get into the moment of the competition of that three-inning game. I did that the whole way."

Wiggins, Gwynn, and Garvey put up another collective zero in the fourth. Horton walked and scored in the top of the fifth, and Tom Herr's run made it 3-0. Horton felt like he was practically toying with the Padres.

In the fifth, Horton finally allowed a baserunner. Martinez walked. But he quickly snuffed out any potential threat, getting Kennedy to hit into a double play before McReynolds grounded out.

"I can't describe it, and my former teammates would laugh at this, but I felt like I was throwing 150 miles an hour," Horton says. "I know I wasn't, but it had so much life. There were times, I can't say it happened very often, where I was standing on the mound thinking, 'Which way do I want to get this guy out?' as opposed to, 'How do I get this guy out?' So that's where I was."

The Cards got Horton two more runs in the top of the sixth, but he stayed locked in just like it was a 1-0 game. Nettles and Templeton flied out, and pinch hitter Luis Salazar grounded out. Two mini-games were complete. And Horton was starting to be aware of what was going on.

"I think I realized it about the fourth or fifth inning," he says. "I came to bat in the fifth inning, and I remember a fan just screaming at me that I had a no-hitter going. In my ear, just, 'You've got a no-hitter going! You know you've got a no-hitter going!' And it's like, all right, I get it. But for me, just to be starting in the big leagues was thrilling, and that kind of experience was just beyond belief."

Andy Hawkins put up a 1-2-3 seventh against St. Louis, and Horton kept picking up steam. He struck out Wiggins, then got Gwynn and Garvey both to ground out. He was six outs away from baseball history.

"It kept building," he says. "I guess I'd say I was not worried about it, not focused on it, because I was thinking more in the moment, of the pitch. A pitcher can focus on the career, you can focus on the year, you can focus on the game, you can focus on the inning, you can focus on the batter and you can focus on the pitch. And the closer you get that progression down to the pitch, the better off you are. In that game, I'd say probably as much as any time in my career I was focused on the pitch for a sustained period of time." He was so focused, in fact, that he missed the incident that makes the game memorable to most who remember it. When the Padres moved from Qualcomm Stadium to new PETCO Park, plenty of stories were shared. But one that came up again and again was the one about Horton, the chicken, and a horse that needed relief.

The Cardinals were kept scoreless in the top of the eighth, and in the middle of the inning, the Padres held a little ceremony on the field. The San Diego Chicken, the team's beloved mascot, was celebrating its 10th anniversary, Horton recalls. Naturally—because what else should a giant chicken do, but ride a horse?—the chicken paraded around the warning track on horseback. It was quite a spectacle. And then it got weirder. The horse dropped a parcel on the warning track, greatly increasing the delay before Horton could resume pitching.

"There's commotion down in the corner, and I have to wait," Horton says. "I didn't even know all that was going on. I didn't feel there was a delay, but I was aware there was something going on. Maybe five minutes was the delay, and they finally get people to get the horse off the field."

Horton, in fact, was probably less fazed by the delay than nearly anyone else in the ballpark. Cards manager Whitey Herzog was livid, seeing gamesmanship at work whether it was actually there or not. Padres manager Dick Williams was mortified by the seeming breach of baseball etiquette. After all, though you never want to be no-hit, you certainly don't want to break it up by distracting the opponent. Baseball's unwritten rules are stricter than the ones that are actually codified. Bush-league tactics are highly frowned upon.

It turns out, of course, that there was nothing nefarious at play. The horse was simply being a horse, and the timing was terrible. Horton didn't think too much of it even after the game.

"The next day, I found out that there was this big hoopla, and that the Chicken almost got fired," Horton says. "Because I had a no-hitter going and he had disrupted me. Dick Williams sent the scorecard over to me and signed it. Dick Williams issued an apology to me because the chicken had messed up my game.

"And Ted, the chicken, comes over to me and has to do a team-[ordered] apology. And I'm like, 'Hey, it's all right, man. No big deal.' So Ted and I became connected over the years because we always had that sense that I got him off the hook for something I didn't even realize was happening."

Still, coincidence or not, it wasn't long before Horton lost his no-hit bid. Martinez struck out for the first out of the eighth, and Kennedy flied out. But McReynolds doubled to left field, ending the no-no. Horton collected himself and got Nettles for the third out, but his chance for immortality had vanished.

"At that point, I had to go, 'I still want to win this game,'" Horton says. "And so there are enough things that kick in quickly enough to where you can't let down."

He permitted a walk and a single in the ninth, but Gwynn grounded into a double play to end the game. Horton was greeted as a hero in the clubhouse, not to mention when he went back to stay with family for the evening.

"I spent the night at my cousin's house, and woke up the next morning and what I remember is her and her husband treating me like a king the next day," he says. "I had breakfast in bed, and they brought me the newspapers with the big stories about the chicken and about my game. It was almost surreal to me, because I couldn't imagine that that would ever happen."

It was a jumping-off point for a young pitcher, and Horton remained in the rotation for the next 2½ months. That turned out to be the longest continuous stint he would ever have as a starter. He went 9-4 on the year and set career highs that he would never equal in wins (nine), innings (125⅔), starts (18), and strikeouts (76).

At that early stage of his career, Horton was learning how to pitch, and how to conduct himself as a major league player. He was also learning how to deal with the media.

"It was my first foray into exposure at a high level," he says. "I didn't have a lot of focus on me, but I sure had a lot of focus on me after that game."

He still views McReynolds' double as a well-hit, clean play, and he doesn't really even have to consider it for long. But it was hit to left field, and the St. Louis left fielder that day was not known as a smooth defender. Lonnie Smith was always speedy, but he carried the nickname "Skates" as a reflection of his less-than-textbook movements in the outfield.

In Horton's mind, he'd made a mistake pitch and paid for it. If you leave a pitch up to a good hitter, it's going to get hit. That's just how it went. But he was confronted by another perspective, as a reporter tried to stir up some trouble. Previously, no member of the press would even have had reason to try to start anything with Horton.

"I remember distinctly a guy asking me if Lonnie Smith should have caught the ball," he remembers. "He said, 'Don't you think Lonnie Smith should have caught that ball?' I said, 'No, it was a changeup that was up a little bit.' It wasn't a bad pitch, and McReynolds was a low-ball hitter and it was about knee-high, top of the knees. Not one of my better changeups. I'd throw it again, but he hit it hard and it hit off the base of the left-field wall. It was a line drive. So I said, 'Nah, that ball was hit hard. Lonnie made an effort to get it. It's not his fault.'"

The line of questioning wasn't over, though.

"The same guy, five minutes later, walks around the other side," Horton recalls, "and says, 'Isn't it true that Lonnie Smith got a bad jump on that ball?' So I said, 'Well, I didn't see the jump on the ball, but that's a hit.' The guy asks me a third time. And it was very informative for me as a rookie to see that I have to be careful about how I present myself and what I say. It's not an anti-media comment, but it's the reality of the sports world. I kind of had a Pollyanna view of sports and people. I tend to be idealistic that way."

Horton handled it smoothly, just as he had the "incident" with the chicken and the horse. One of Horton's best qualities, as a player and a broadcaster, has always been his affability. He nodded, smiled, and moved on.

If Horton was in any jeopardy of getting cocky after his big game, he was brought back to earth quickly. He pitched a fine game his next time out, holding the Giants to two runs over seven innings. But in his last start of the lengthy road trip, the Dodgers drilled him. Horton got three outs in that game before he was lifted for a pinch-hitter. He was charged with five runs on seven hits and even committed two balks.

"I went to L.A., the last start before the All-Star Game, and I got beat around pretty good," he recalls. "Steve Sax hit a [single] on the first pitch of the game, and it got worse from there. I got humbled."

Never again would he find himself quite so on top of the baseball world, either. At least not individually. The two-hitter stood for the rest of Horton's career as easily his best game as a big leaguer. It was his only shutout and one of just three complete games. Nonetheless, he did draw on his big day as he went forward in his career. Once he'd pitched that game, he realized what he was capable of. Even if he didn't reach those heights again, he had the confidence to know it was possible.

"I think it does linger," he says. "Even that [Los Angeles] start, if I'd had that start without the start before, as a rookie I might have said, 'Maybe this league's too hard for me.' It ends up giving you a perspective on how hard it is to do that."

And yet to some extent, Horton still marvels at how good he was for one day.

"People say, 'I don't understand how a guy can have such a bad game after he's done so well,'" he says. "And I think as an athlete looking back, you realize it's harder to understand how you can perform at that high level. If you look at it that way, this is tough to do. But when you're there, you enjoy it and you try to make it last as long as you can. You know there's a leveling off that eventually happens. You can't get too high when you have those games, and you can't get too low."

His teammates assured him there would be more, but the truth is, most pitchers only get one chance at immortality—if that.

"The one I remember the most is [Bruce] Sutter, because I had been in the bullpen with him and I admired him tremendously," Horton says. "So I remember him being one of the guys that came up to me and congratulated me. Bob Forsch was another one. The typical thing they said, and I heard it a couple of different times, was, 'You'll have your chance to get another one.' I don't know whether they went in the corner of the room and said, 'No he won't,' but that's kind of the typical thing."

Horton did play on two St. Louis pennant winners, but by '85 he'd been permanently cast as somewhere between a full-time reliever and a swingman between the bullpen and the rotation. He made three starts for the '85 Cardinals, nine in '86, and six in '87. Horton pitched in nine postseason games for the Cards. He had to leave, however, to win a ring. Horton was traded to the White Sox in 1988 in a deal that netted the Cardinals Jose DeLeon. In August of '88 he was flipped again, this time to the Dodgers.

When Los Angeles upset the Mets in the NLCS that year, it made three World Series trips in four years for Horton. He didn't pitch in the Fall Classic, but he did get to play on a team that won it all. Still, despite the team success, personal stardom never found him. He hit the pinnacle in his 19th appearance.

"You have no sense while you're doing it of how . . . that's it," Horton says. "That is the moment. You're having your moment. I'm sure Bud Smith looks back and feels the same way, and Jose Jimenez looks back and says, 'That was the pinnacle of my career, but I actually had it as a rookie.' A lot of good team things happened after that, but . . ."

He was never the story of the day in that same way again. Then again, to have it even once is something that not everyone can claim. Horton realizes that, and the entire day still brings a smile to his face. It wasn't just his best game. It was his best day as a ballplayer.

"I think it was the other stuff," he says. "I think it was being a rookie, staying with my cousin, some of the hoopla around it. Plus, it was near perfection. And I think I've had opportunities to remember it in the subsequent years. I just think about, 'Wow, I did that.' I think the reality of what I had done hit me more afterward. And I mean years afterward."

CHAPTER 15

SCOTT ROLEN

Roger Clemens had read the scouting reports, and more importantly, he'd seen them play out in front of him. Although Scott Rolen was a perennial All-Star and a dangerous slugger—even an MVP candidate in 2004—there was a well-established book on Rolen. Pitch him up and in, and hard, and you'll get him out. He can't catch up to that stuff even when he's healthy, let alone when he's hurting. If ever there was a scouting report written to Clemens' liking, that was it. Clemens had a devastating split-finger fastball and could do plenty of other things with plenty of other pitches. But the proud native Texan always loved to come at hitters with the high, hard stuff. If they heard the seams of the ball go whistling past, so much the better.

He'd done it throughout Game 7 of the '04 National League Championship Series, not just to Rolen but to the rest of the Cardinals, with great success. Earlier in the series, and earlier in the year, Clemens had made the Cardinals look silly with splitters. But at make-or-break time, Clemens leaned on his signature pitch: the gas. Clemens had left the Yankees to come to the Astros the previous winter, with the goal of turning Houston from a playoff team into a championship team. He was signed not only for his ability but his attitude, his pitching smarts, and his guts. He was certain that his best was better than your best, and his best was always the fastball.

Rolen knew all of that too. He just didn't care. Video and printouts were of little interest to him. He wanted the chance to go toe-to-toe with Clemens and see how he measured up. So in the biggest at-bat of Rolen's life, the at-bat that was the very reason Clemens had come to Houston, the Hall of Famer challenged the slugger. And the slugger answered the challenge emphatically.

Rolen knew it was a mistake before the ball even left Clemens' hand. He knew it before Clemens even began his delivery. Rolen knew—he didn't believe, he knew—that the Astros were making a mistake if they let Clemens throw any pitch to him. Hitting had always been hard for Rolen, even when it was going well. So this was not a familiar feeling. But he had no doubt that it was the truth.

Never mind that Clemens hadn't thrown his 90th pitch of the night, that he was still reaching the mid-90s with his fastball and showing no signs of fatigue. Never mind that a dangerous left-handed hitter with a sense of the dramatic was on deck in Jim Edmonds. Never mind that Rolen hadn't felt physically right for more than six weeks. Rolen was certain that if the Astros let Clemens come after him, he would deliver.

Much to Rolen's delight, that's just what manager Phil Garner did. Garner stayed with his horse, his legend. He trusted Roger Clemens to do what Roger Clemens had done best for 20 years—to make the big pitch in the big situation. This time, Clemens didn't get it done. Rolen beat him, and sent the Cardinals to the World Series for the first time in 17 years. Rolen's two-run, two-out, sixth-inning home run provided the tie-breaking, and ultimately winning, runs in a 4-2 St. Louis victory. He hit a pitch that often gave him fits, off a Hall of Fame pitcher who gave everyone fits. And he knew it was going to happen.

"It wasn't approach, it wasn't anything [like that]," Rolen remembers. "It was downright competitiveness. It was, 'I am going to beat you. Right now. I don't know how. I don't care how. You don't know how. I don't know what you're going to throw or how you're going to throw it.' And it happened on the first pitch. I have a ton of respect for Roger Clemens. And the thing for me was that I out-competed one of the most competitive people in the world. That's the success."

Rolen rarely relished at-bats against Clemens. "Not a comfortable

With one swing, Scott Rolen erased more than a month of frustration that plagued him at the end of 2004 and early in that year's postseason. *AP/WWP*

at-bat," he'd sometimes say about dominating power pitchers. But in this case, facing Clemens helped Rolen do what he needed to. For six games, St. Louis and Houston had played fierce, brilliant, beautiful, draining baseball in the National League Championship Series. The series took place out of baseball's spotlight, thanks to Boston's historic comeback against the Yankees in the American League Championship Series. But for sheer quality of baseball, it was every bit the equal of, if not superior to, the ALCS.

"I will never play in a better baseball series or better baseball games than that," Rolen said, echoing a sentiment held by many who played in the series. "They had an unbelievable, professional team. As did we. Talented, experienced, professional. It doesn't get any better than that."

The heavily favored, 105-win Redbirds were a juggernaut. They had finished 13 games ahead of the division rival Astros in the regular season, and nine games better than any other team in the National League. They had put the National League Central away before August even started. So when St. Louis took Games 1 and 2 at home, talk began that the series might be over before it even returned to Busch Stadium. But that was far from how it turned out.

Clemens and the Astros won Game 3 at Minute Maid Park, with Clemens shutting down Rolen and the potent lineup around him— a lineup that led the National League in runs, batting average, and slugging percentage that year. The Astros came from behind to win Game 4 at home, salting the victory with a Carlos Beltran home run. It was such a tough loss to take that Julian Tavarez, who permitted Beltran's long ball, bashed a dugout phone and broke a bone in his hand. Game 5? Simply a modern classic, decided when Jeff Kent hit a three-run walk-off homer to break a scoreless tie in the ninth.

Stunned but not quite staggered, the Cardinals came home just hoping to force a Game 7. The Astros were riding high, and the Cards weren't sure exactly what had happened to their lead—or what might be about to happen to their season. It took St. Louis 12 innings and a remember-where-you-were-when-it-happened walk-off homer from Jim Edmonds to ensure that the season would last one more game. The Cardinals could still see their season end, but they could also extend it by one more series.

"It wasn't yours to win the night before because you couldn't win," said Rolen. "Now you can win. So when you can win it with one game, no matter what happens, it puts you in a better spot. Without question. But Roger Clemens is on the mound. And that's their best chance to win. Going into Game 7, I thought, the outcome of today's game is OK either way, because we both earned the chance to play in the World Series. If they would have beaten us 2-1, I'd have been fine, because they earned that. Just as we did. My preference was the way it turned out. But it was that good to me, that good a competition."

With Clemens on the mound for the visiting Astros, Rolen and his teammates knew the competition would reach a level that even great players seldom experience. Clemens was already a 300-game winner, a milestone he reached against St. Louis a year earlier. He was also already a two-time World Series champion and a five-time pennant-winner. Clemens, more than anyone else on the field that night, knew what it took to win a championship. But Rolen had an idea, too.

He shared his idea, simple as it was, in the Cardinals' daily hitters' meeting with manager Tony La Russa and hitting coach Mitchell Page. Day after day, the Cards had held meetings to go over strategy, tactics, game planning, and scouting reports. A flood of information suited some players beautifully, but seemed overwhelming—or superfluous—to others. Place Rolen in the "less is more" camp.

"We go to Game 7, Roger Clemens on the mound, and we all saunter into our meeting," Rolen remembers. "Every day, every pitcher, every day—going over relievers that we faced the night before, starters that we faced four days before that. And so we go into this meeting. I got a feel when we were in there, and I kind of felt the way I believed everybody else was feeling. I think Tony said, 'Anybody have anything to say about Clemens?'

"And I waited about as long as I could before Mitch or somebody started talking. And I just said, 'I do. We're facing one of the best, most competitive pitchers in the history of baseball tonight in Game 7 of the National League Championship Series. We need to go out and out-compete him or we are not going to win. I don't care if he throws a fastball, curveball, split, cutter. It doesn't matter. We have to go into the box and we have to out-compete him tonight. Because he will be out-competing us. If we don't, we will not win. Our chance is to out-compete one of the most competitive, successful pitchers in baseball.' And I don't know who it was, but somebody clapped his hands and said, 'Let's go.' And we all walked out of the room."

The Cardinals dug in from the start against Clemens, but for five innings it didn't matter. He was Roger Clemens, and he was rolling. Craig Biggio led off the game with a home run, and an Edmonds error brought home the second Houston run. Edmonds had made a brilliant play on Brad Ausmus to save runs in the second, but it merely kept the lead from getting larger. A sacrifice fly cut the margin to 2-1, but after 5½ innings Houston still led. Clemens was on his game, and the no-name but extremely effective Astros bullpen was looming. The greatest Cardinals regular season in decades was 12 outs from ending without so much as a pennant, never mind a world championship.

In the sixth, Cards starter Jeff Suppan was lifted for a pinch-hitter, Clemens-killer Roger Cedeno. Relegated to a supporting role at best by that point in the year, Cedeno was still a trump card for La Russa, thanks to his 11-for-25 career mark against Clemens. The move worked, as Cedeno singled, then took second on a sacrifice. After Larry Walker grounded out, though, Clemens was an out away from escaping. He got ahead of Albert Pujols, 1-2, but Pujols punished Clemens for throwing a fastball up and over the plate. The superstar's double tied the game, and brought up Rolen.

With Edmonds, a left-hander, on deck, Garner and the Astros had a decision, but not much of one. Rolen hadn't been at his best since an early-September calf injury. He was also dealing with knee issues, and there was also that matter of the high-and-tight fastball that was Clemens' calling card. Undoubtedly, Garner also considered the fact that Edmonds had just burned the Astros a night earlier. No Cardinal had broken the hearts of the Astros and their fans more times than Edmonds.

Despite Rolen's solid numbers against Clemens for his career, the third baseman was definitely the hitter to go after. The open base was a non-factor. Given a choice between Rolen and Edmonds, Garner chose Rolen, and few people would question the decision. It was a mistake, though—even if Rolen was the only person at Busch Stadium who knew it.

"I don't have a King Kong mentality when I play baseball," he said. "I have a very realistic perspective on things. If I struggle off a pitcher, I'm not afraid to know that I may go 0-for-4 before the game starts, and then try to cut into that. And so this story is different from my mentality, the way I approach the game. Because [at the time], I'm saying in my mind, to myself, 'If you leave him in, you've lost. You need to walk me. You should walk me. If you don't, you lose.' I'm telling myself this. I'm speaking in my mind to them. I'm not convincing myself. I know this for a fact. I don't know why or how. And that's not the way I think.

"And so as I'm on deck, these are the thoughts in my mind. 'I'm going to get you.' It wasn't a positive reinforcement thing, and it wasn't 'Let me at him, let me at him.' It was almost, in my mind, a fact. If they brought another pitcher in, all bets are off; I don't have any idea what's going to happen. But I'm just thinking at the time, 'If you leave him in, you're going to lose.'

"As I walked in, the last thought in my mind was, 'You just lost.' I wasn't thinking fastball. I wasn't thinking split. I wasn't thinking anything in the count. I got in the box and I wasn't swinging the bat well in general. And I got in the box and he threw a ball that I, nine times out of 10, can't handle. First pitch, the ball was a fastball up and in, and I don't handle that ball very well. So I squared the ball up on the barrel, and I knew as soon as I hit it that I had just won the game for the St. Louis Cardinals to send us to the World Series. As the ball came off my bat, I hit it and I knew at that time, 'You lost. I just won the game for the St. Louis Cardinals to go to the World Series.'"

It was sweet for so many reasons. It was sweet simply because it was the National League pennant. It was sweet because it was the rival Astros, and the Hall of Famer Clemens. It was sweet because of the quality of the preceding six games. It was sweet because Rolen had been injured and unable to play in his only previous NLCS, in 2002. And it was sweet because Rolen had seen his finest season compromised a month and a half earlier. On his way to a possible MVP award, Rolen sustained a serious left calf injury in a game at Dodger Stadium in September.

The pain hindered him. The loss of a vital timing mechanism—balancing on his front leg at the plate—crippled his production. Rolen went 3-for-18 in the last week of the season after returning from the injury. He was 0-for-12 in the Division Series. He ran into two homers earlier in the NLCS, but he wasn't feeling right even then. Just as he put aside everything else, he shoved the injury aside as well. If Clemens couldn't keep Rolen from winning the game, a calf injury couldn't either.

"I spent the last week and a half of the season uncompetitive, trying to get at-bats to have a chance," he said. "That's the way I entered the playoffs. I entered the playoffs, in my mind, in an uncompetitive physical shape. Everything I did all year was gone at the end of the season, after that [injury]. I was getting some hits. I didn't get a hit in the Division Series, and then it starts compounding. I was swinging a little better in the LCS, but not with the consistency."

So in addition to the bad matchup against the dominating, legendary pitcher, add a physical barrier as well. But if Clemens' ability made the feat harder, his presence, his competitiveness and his résumé made Rolen more able to accomplish it.

"I think the fact that that guy was out there helped bring that out," Rolen said. "I think that Roy Oswalt would have brought that out. Jake Peavy brings that out. Greg Maddux brings that out. These guys are competitive guys. And if you are not equal or greater in your competitive mindset, you are going to get beat.

"That was the idea in my mind of the whole hitters' meeting thing. This is no joke. It doesn't matter what he throws, guys. This is one of the most competitive people in the world, and he will beat us. He will beat you if you do not give him all that he can handle. And I thoroughly believe that.

"Many times I've gone out against Roger Clemens or Roy Oswalt or whomever with a great competitive mindset and, uh-uh, it isn't going to happen. But if you don't go out that way, no chance. And that was my point in the meeting. That was the only thing I wanted to get across. Guys, this is it. There are no tricks here. There's no numbers. There's no stats. There's no nothing. This is what's inside."

Somewhere in Rolen's mind, he knew he hadn't hit a walk-off home run. But it wasn't in the front of his brain. The logical part of his brain was aware that his team still needed nine outs to secure the National League championship. Logic was drowned out a bit, however. Sometimes you just know. Rolen knew. It was such a certainty that he still doesn't remember the remainder of the game. It's a blur, if the images exist at all.

"When I crossed home plate, in my mind, there wasn't a question," he said. "We were going to the World Series. I really don't remember a pitch after that. I don't remember anything about it, except the win."

The images that remain are from later that night. Jason Isringhausen pitched a 1-2-3 ninth, cementing hero status for all 25 Cardinals, but especially Rolen, Pujols, Edmonds, and Suppan. They had beaten Clemens. They had beaten the ferocious Astros. They had taken a World Series-starved fan base to the Fall Classic for the first time since 1987. They all knew how special it was. Many of them, including Rolen, had been there for previous disappointments. Most recent was 2002, when an injury to Rolen helped cement a defeat against the Giants in the NLCS.

"I remember standing at second base with Mike Matheny," Rolen said. "Hugging each other, jumping up and down. And I remember telling him, 'Look at this. Don't ever forget this. You and I, remind each other. Let's not forget this scene.'"

It is not spoiled now, not even by the frustration that followed in the World Series. The Cardinals were swept, and embarrassed, by the Red Sox in a series that started less than 48 hours later. Rolen and Edmonds failed to come through with the bases loaded and the score tied in the eighth inning of Game 1, a missed opportunity that allowed the Red Sox to win the game in the bottom of the same inning. It was the only time the Cardinals were even factors in the series. That defeat stung badly, and it was mystifying. After they reached so deep and accomplished so much in the NLCS, how could they fall so short in the World Series?

"I believe it to this day—that's why I don't even like to talk about baseball anymore, because I don't know what the hell I'm talking about—if I wasn't going to win a World Series in 2004, I wasn't going to win one," Rolen said, as baffled by his team's 2006 title as by its '04 runner-up showing. "I didn't know what it took. After we got swept by the Red Sox, I went home and said, 'I don't know what it takes to win a world championship if that didn't do it.'"

But the more time that passes, the more the World Series fades— and the more one at-bat shines.

"I'm running around the bases," Rolen remembers, as though it were an hour ago. "I'm not a guy that has my arms up running around the bases. And all I could think about rounding first was my arm going up in the air. And it didn't. It didn't. I couldn't. There was so much emotion inside of me. I'm down at first base, and it was like I heard the crowd go from the excitement from Albert's double to one pitch later, another world. I felt that. What an unbelievable outpouring of everything."

Rolen's Cardinals story, like his 2004 story, does not end on a happy note. A divide with La Russa that started in 2005 grew irreparable by the end of 2007, and following the 2007 season, he was traded to Toronto. It was a difficult split for Rolen, who hoped to end his career in St. Louis. But when he looks back, he thinks of the high points, like winning the 2006 World Series, and beating the Astros in 2004. One relationship does not define his time wearing a Cardinals uniform.

"I loved it there," he said. "My wife loved it there. I think it's the greatest place to play baseball in the game. The atmosphere, the fans, the city, the celebration of the baseball. I'd recommend it to anybody. I cherish the memories that I have there. Won a world championship. We had success. I can't say enough good things about it."

CHAPTER 16

ANDY BENES

When Andy Benes tells the story of his last game in the major leagues, he starts two years earlier. Retirement first threatened Benes when he didn't even realize it, in the form of a knee injury that rendered him a shell of the power pitcher he once was. Benes raged against the end, though. Pitching practically on one leg, he capped the 2000 campaign with a valiant performance in the National League Championship Series.

He underwent surgery on the troublesome right knee after the postseason, but simply wasn't right when the '01 season started. Operating with a battered body and a diminished arsenal, Benes lurched to a 7.38 ERA in 27 games in 2001. Three home runs in a relief appearance on August 20th, his 34th birthday, made it perfectly clear how far Benes had fallen.

That's when retirement actually entered Benes' mind—but only as a hint, a mention in passing from his manager. Tony La Russa approached Benes on the field soon after that birthday debacle, and La Russa told Benes that the pitcher needed to decide whether his time had come. Benes decided he wasn't ready to hang up his spikes, but the reality of his situation was becoming clearer.

"His whole theme was, you really need to decide if you want to keep playing or not," Benes says. "He said a lot of guys play past when they're really able to play. A guy he brought up was [Dennis] Eckersley, who just loved the game and played until he was past 40. He said, 'If you're not really up for that, that's OK. It's OK to shut it down now. You've had a nice career.' So I really thought about that."

Benes believed he had one last run left. He pitched only twice more in '01 before more knee surgery ended his season. But he got ready, got healthy, and came back the following spring ready for one more shot. Soon after that, retirement was all but forced upon him. A terrible start to the 2002 regular season left Benes without a team. The Cardinals gave Benes a choice: retire or be cut. And though player and team settled on a third option, a lengthy disabled list stint, Benes knew he wasn't wanted.

And still, something churned inside him. Something told him that the time wasn't quite right. He was sitting at home, not even coming to the ballpark, but part of Benes was still in the Cardinals clubhouse.

"The TV would be on, and sometimes the Cardinals games would be on," he remembers. "I was watching a lot of these younger guys pitch over the course of the month, and I just remember my attitude was not right. I still felt like I was better than they were, even though statistically I wasn't."

As a matter of fact, Benes did show that he was better than a lot of those kids. He worked his way back from the pitching mound of a tee-ball game to Busch Stadium, and added a stirring final act to his 14-season career. Finally, though, Benes knew this time was really it. After fighting retirement for more than a year, he finally accepted it. Not, however, before he took a turn as the Cardinals' knight in shining knee brace. And not before he discovered an out pitch that he considered not only a weapon but a blessing.

A team starved for starting pitching help turned to Benes after scads of other options failed. Remarkably, he was more than just a fallback, not simply a seat-filler. He thrived. Benes made 15 appearances after he went home, and he put up a superb 1.86 ERA. The Cardinals went 10-5 in those games, and a team that had been reeling instead roared to the postseason. In the end, baseball didn't tell Benes that he was done. He told baseball he'd had enough, and that's all any player can ask.

Not many players get to go out on their own terms. When Andy Benes got the chance, he knew he had to seize it. *AP/WWP*

"I was able to leave the game with no regrets," he says proudly. "And I can say that there has not been one day when I thought, 'Man, I really wish I could go out there.' I haven't missed it. I feel blessed to have been able to play the amount of time that I did."

The 2002 season, Benes' last year, stands as one of the most memorable in Cardinal history—for many wonderful reasons and just as many awful ones. It's a year when the Cards won 97 games and soared to the National League Central title by 13 games over second-place Houston. It's the year in which they acquired team cornerstone Scott Rolen from Philadelphia in one of the franchise's best trades, and the year when they knocked off the defending World Series champion Diamondbacks in three games in the Division Series.

It's also the year when the organization was rocked by the shocking and heartbreaking death of star pitcher and team leader Darryl Kile. And Kile's passing came only four days after the loss of franchise icon and Hall of Fame broadcaster Jack Buck. On the field, the Cardinals went through 14 starting pitchers on the year and 10 in April alone. Even before the loss of Kile, it was one of La Russa and pitching coach Dave Duncan's great jobs simply to keep the pitching staff from disintegrating.

"Of those 10 pitchers," Benes jokes, "a bunch of them had to not do well for me to get back in the mix. I hated it for them. I never wanted to have an opportunity because somebody else failed. I wanted to have an opportunity because I was doing well. But those were the circumstances, and I was able to go and do my job."

The 2001 season had been a slog for Benes, but when '02 started, he was filled with optimism. He felt good physically for the first time in a long time. And though nothing was promised to him in terms of a job, Benes liked his chances in Spring Training. He did all he could to force his way into the Cardinals rotation. Benes made only two starts out of six spring appearances, pitching in "piggyback" fashion with Kile. Recuperating from shoulder surgery, Kile was handled gently. So after Kile pitched in a game, Benes would follow him.

It's not easy for a starting pitcher to relieve. Starters are routine-driven individuals, and the uncertainty of pitching out of the bullpen can be jarring. Benes made the most of it, though, putting up a 2.35 ERA in 23 spring innings. He earned a spot at the back of the Cardinals rotation.

"My spring," he says, "was one of the best springs I ever had."

The good feeling didn't last long, however. In his first regular-season start, Benes walked four and allowed two homers in four innings as the Cards fell to Colorado, 6-1. He was chased after three innings and four more walks in his second start. Game three, a 14-5 loss in Arizona, was an unmitigated disaster, as he allowed 10 runs—but only three earned. Questions bubbled up as to whether Benes was finished.

"It was after that game," Benes says, "that I really started thinking, 'Hey, is this what I'm supposed to be doing?' I mentioned it to some of my teammates, like, 'I don't know if I should keep trying this or what.' I felt like I was throwing hard enough and I had good enough stuff. I just felt like it came down to locating and how much my heart was in it."

Benes wasn't the only one wondering. A day later, he recalls, general manager Walt Jocketty approached him. The choice presented to Benes was stark and unpleasant: retire or be released.

"I told them I needed to talk to my agent [Scott Boras], and that I'd let them know," Benes says. "I talked to Scott, and he said, 'No, just have them release you, because if somebody else wants you to play for them, then you have that opportunity. If you retire, you don't have that opportunity.'"

After the conversation with Boras, Benes informed the Cardinals that he was willing to accept his release. To everyone's benefit, however, a third option was found.

"I [still] had trouble with my right knee," Benes notes, "and they eventually put me on the disabled list, which they could do because I had an injury. They told me to go ahead and take it home and kind of leave it at that."

So after 13 years as a pitcher, it was time for Benes to be dad for a while. He found he liked the work, even if he wasn't ready to quit his other job. "I was home for a month," he says. "I was a husband and a dad. I was watching baseball practice and going to my kids' events. I did absolutely nothing baseball-wise. I didn't pick up a baseball. I didn't condition. Nothing. I just assumed I was done."

So did the Cardinals, at least for a while. But as the season went on, both sides realized they might benefit from a reunion. The Cardinals were staying above water with their makeshift rotation, but they weren't thriving. And Benes still had the itch.

"I called Walt, and I said, 'Listen, you guys are paying me a lot of money to be at home, and your pitchers are struggling right now. I really think I can help you, but you guys have got to want me to try. Let me know if you want me to start working out and getting my arm back in shape. I can go rehab and see what happens.' Walt said, 'I'll let you know.' A week later, he calls me and says, 'What are you doing?' And I said, 'Well, actually, I'm pitching right now.'

"He said, 'Great, because we talked to Tony and Dunc and some of the other people in the organization, and they want you to start working out. Who are you pitching to?' And I said, 'My six-year-old's tee-ball team.' And being the general manager and kind of a witty guy, he said, 'Well, are you getting them out?' And I said, 'Actually, I'm hitting their bats, so that's good. I'm aiming the ball really nice right now.'"

With the club beginning a lengthy homestand, Benes could come to the park and work out with bullpen catcher Jeff Murphy. But at first, Murphy was the only person watching Benes pitch. Benes wondered if his comeback attempt was even being taken seriously. Finally he got the call to go to the minor leagues and begin pitching competitively. He reported to Triple-A Memphis, but even then Benes was unsure whether his job was as a big-league pitcher-in-waiting or as a second pitching coach for the kids.

Benes tried not to think too much about it, and to enjoy the chance to pitch competitively anywhere, at any level. He headed to Memphis, and chose to make the most of it. Rather than commuting, as some rehabbing major leaguers do, Benes made a temporary home at AutoZone Park. He also found himself pitching on the same day as Kile once again. His first Triple-A start was on June 18, the same day Kile pitched the Cardinals into first place in a game against the Angels. He even got Kile's uniform number.

"They gave me No. 57," Benes remembers. "And I was like, 'This is really weird. What a terrible number.' I was talking to DK and I said, 'This is a horrible number. I don't know how you kept this number.' But I had that number, and I was also pitching on the same day that DK was pitching in the big leagues."

Five days later, Benes and Kile were scheduled to start on the same day once again—Kile at Wrigley Field, and Benes in Memphis against Tucson. Kile's start never came.

"I was in my hotel room, and I was waiting to go to the ballpark one day," Benes says. "I was waiting for the Cardinal-Cub game to come on and it was canceled because DK had passed away. And I knew right then.

"My wife was with me. She had come down for a few days to hang out with me. And I knew right then that I was going to have a chance. I knew that I was going to finish out the season and I was there to be his backup guy. I had followed him in Spring Training, and we had been good buddies for a long time. I knew that there were just too many things that added up for me to be that guy that finished out the season."

The loss devastated Benes and the Cardinals. But as Benes envisioned, it also meant an opportunity. He had to keep toiling in the minors, but after three more starts he was back in the bigs. The Cards had no idea what they'd get from Benes, but they were pitching-starved enough to give him the ball in the fifth game after the All-Star break. He lasted only four innings, but he kept the game close and St. Louis went on to win at Dodger Stadium, 9-2. Benes didn't know where the ride was going to go. But he finally knew when it was going to end.

"I felt like I was going to finish out the season for DK," he says. "And I really knew at that point. I was fortunate to be playing, but I knew it was going to be my last season. It wasn't like I thought, 'Well, if I come back and pitch well, I'll be able to play next year.' I knew it was going to be my last season regardless."

The Cardinals bolstered their rotation but put Benes in limbo just three days later. They traded for Chuck Finley, adding a veteran left-hander to their starting five. Benes pitched in relief the next day while La Russa and Duncan pondered where he fit in the team's plans. Four days after pitching out of the bullpen, he made his longest start of the year—a modest 4⅔ innings, but it was still progress. Benes fanned five Giants and issued just two walks, his fewest in a start in '02.

Events were turning his way. And though Finley's arrival first seemed like a roadblock for Benes, it soon became a boon. In a rare case of lefty-righty transference, Finley showed Benes the pitch that would help make him one of baseball's best stories over the final two months of 2002. Finley showed Benes a grip for a split-finger fastball, a pitch Benes had never thrown before. Benes liked the pitch. He got movement on it, and he could control where it went. He knew he was on to something, even if he had to convince Duncan.

"I said, 'Hey, I have a new pitch,'" Benes recalls. "And he said, 'If I had a nickel for every time I had heard that in my career, I probably would have doubled my salary.' But I started throwing the split-finger in the bullpen, and it actually looked pretty good. So I said, 'I think I might try to throw it in the game if the situation comes up where it's not going to hurt me. I'll maybe give it a shot.' And he said, 'Yeah, just pick your spot.' And that was kind of the end of it."

In Benes' next start, against Florida, he tried the pitch out. But he didn't exactly wait for a safe situation. With the bases loaded and no outs in the second inning, he fired a splitter—and got a comebacker double play. An inning later, he got Derrek Lee to hit into a 6-4-3 twin killing. A new Benes, a pitcher with a shiny new offering, was born.

"When I came off the field," Benes says, "[Duncan] said, 'What pitch did you throw?' I said, 'That was my new pitch!' And I was real excited about it. He said, 'I told you to throw it when it wasn't going to hurt you.'

"I said, 'Listen, when you have the bases loaded and nobody out, whatever I was throwing before wasn't getting them out either.' So you might as well take a risk. And I did, and from that point on, that pitch just kept getting better and better for me."

Benes lasted 6⅓ shutout innings that night. Five days later, he struck out eight and held the powerful Braves to one run in 7⅓ innings. By that time his ERA, once in the double digits, had dropped to a respectable 4.58. And he was just getting started. All the while, Benes was growing less and less concerned about petty worries like whether he was starting or relieving, or what place he held in the rotation. Once he saw the end in sight, his perspective changed.

"I knew things were going to be good when I got done, and they had already sent me home once because I wasn't good enough," he recalls. "If they sent me home again, hey, I knew things were good. So I was just like, 'I retired once, what's the big deal?' and I think because of that attitude, my pride and my ego kind of got thrown out the door."

So he was having fun, and he was rolling. In Benes' 15 appearances after his semi-retirement, his ERA dropped 14 times. The only time it climbed was a September 11 game against Milwaukee, when it blipped up from 3.18 to 3.30. Benes became one of the best stories on a team full of remarkable stories, and the Cardinals ran away with the division. Kile's last start was the game that put them in first place to stay. Benes took the baton and helped his team run to the finish.

The late-summer surge provided Benes with some scrapbook individual moments, too. On September 6, he started against his younger brother Alan for the first time in his career. Andy went the distance, striking out six in an 11-2 win. Alan struggled, allowing eight runs and not surviving the third inning.

"We were just a lot better than the Cubs were," the elder Benes says modestly.

It was his last major league win but not his last highlight. He entered the final day of the season with 1,998 strikeouts, needing two for a milestone. The Cards also needed the game, since a win and an Arizona loss would have given St. Louis home-field advantage in the first round of the playoffs. Benes got strikeout No. 1,999 on batter No. 1 of the game. Then he waited.

"I looked over at my buddies and I was like, 'I need one more.' So I figured, that'll be easy enough. But we get to the fifth inning, and I was having back spasms, which I had a little trouble with. My right knee was bad so my back got out of line. But it happened that the last guy I faced, I struck the guy out."

The Cardinals won, but so did Arizona, and so they headed west to Bank One Ballpark for the Division Series. They went up 2-0 in the series, and closed out the sweep in Game 3 with Benes a bit shaky. It was on to the NLCS for the second time in three years.

This time, though, St. Louis fell behind 2-0. Finley pitched and won Game 3, but the Cards were still in trouble when Benes took the hill for Game 4 at Pac Bell Park. Benes knew that unless he won, and his teammates got hot, he would be making his last appearance in a major league game. The offense handed Benes two runs in the top of the first, an auspicious start. He allowed two men to reach in the bottom of the inning, but dodged trouble, and from there he locked in. Benes retired nine in a row before a Benito Santiago walk in the fourth, and had put down 13 of 15 when the fifth started.

Still leading 2-0, he struck out Rich Aurilia to open the sixth. But Jeff Kent walked in front of the menacing Barry Bonds, about the last outcome Benes would have wanted. He walked Bonds—and then he was out of the game. If Benes knew he was pitching the last game of his last season, he was blindsided when he found out he had faced his last batter. It was about the only regret he had from the entire remarkable run.

"I walk him and get the ball back from Mike (Matheny), and all of a sudden, here comes Tony," Benes recalls. "I was at the back of the mound, and I look up, and here comes Tony. This is the second trip, which means that I'm out of the game. And I'm like, 'Oh my gosh, you've got to be kidding me.' It totally caught me off guard. And I remember thinking, if I would have known that, I would have thrown strikes to Barry Bonds."

Instead, he was lifted for reliever Rick White, who had been brilliant for the Cardinals since signing as a released free agent in August. White struck out Santiago for the second out, but J. T. Snow's two-out double tied the game. Benes could not win the game, though his team still had a chance. Benes had hope, but the reality of the situation was daunting. As he walked off the field, he took a moment to appreciate his surroundings.

"I remember waving to [my wife]," he says, "and just thinking, 'This hopefully is not the last time, but it could be the last time I ever come out here. And if it is, it was a pretty good game.'"

White held the fort in the seventh, and came out again for the eighth. He retired the first two batters, then walked Bonds intentionally, making Santiago his 10th batter faced. White didn't benefit from the same quick hook that claimed Benes, and the decision turned out poorly. Given a second look at the veteran reliever, Santiago took him deep for a 4-2 Giants lead.

St. Louis picked up a run in the ninth but still fell, 4-3. A day later, the Cardinals' season was over. So was Benes' career. The series defeat was heartbreaking for the Cardinals, who had overcome so much. To this day, La Russa ranks the 2002 loss as perhaps the most crushing of his time in St. Louis. And for Benes, it went double.

"You only know what's going on with your team, so you think that you're a team of destiny," he said. "But the Giants probably thought they were the same thing for different reasons. But with the tragedy that had gone on, and the fact that we had to really work hard to get to the playoffs, then we faced Randy Johnson and Curt Schilling against Arizona. We faced those guys and won the Division Series. I think we all thought that we were going to be able to win. And it just didn't happen. I think that made it a lot more difficult to handle."

Not that he ever had a second thought. Benes knew all along that he was making his last tour of the bigs. And though he had hoped it would last about seven more games, he had no doubt that 162 more would be asking far too much. He went home again, this time for good. And he still treasures being able to go out his way. Benes views the entire experience, and the pitch that helped him go so far, as a gift from above.

"I just know that the Lord blessed me with that," he said. "I have a strong faith, and I really felt like that was something he blessed me with to finish my career. People in the community and just people talking to me in general, they remember how I finished. I was able to leave on a really good note as opposed to pitching bad and getting sent home.

"I really feel like the Lord gave me a second chance and blessed me with that pitch. I was playing catch with my son after the season was over, and I had just gotten done being able to throw that thing however I wanted to, and once the season was over, it was like I didn't have any feel for it or really know how I could throw it anymore. Even playing catch, it was like I had it and then I didn't have it. It was really cool, that's why I say I really felt like it was a gift to pitch out the year and end on a good note."

CHAPTER 17

KEN REITZ

Some young players need a kick in the pants to get going. Some require a pat on the back. Ken Reitz just needed a little home cooking.

Reitz played in 11 major league seasons. He won a Gold Glove and played in an All-Star Game. He hit well in the minor leagues, and rapped out a .359 batting average in his 21-game major league debut in 1972. But early in '73, he was struggling, and Reitz's spot on the Cardinals' roster was no sure thing.

When the Redbirds left for the West Coast for a three-city road trip early in '73, Reitz was batting an anemic .177. And though batting average doesn't always tell the story of a hitter's contributions, in this case it wasn't the slightest bit misleading. Reitz carried a .227 on-base percentage and a .194 slugging percentage. He went from April 11 to April 29 without an RBI. The young third baseman was well regarded for his defense, but even top-flight catchers and shortstops have to swing the bat better than Reitz was managing early in '73.

"I came up in '72 and I did really well," Reitz recalls. "Then, in '73, I was the Opening Day third baseman in Pittsburgh, the year after Roberto Clemente died. And I got a hit the first time up, then I went into a [1-for-18] slump. I started getting a few hits here, a few hits there, but they were probably going to send me back down to the minor leagues.

"[Manager] Red Schoendienst talked to me, and Bing Devine, who was the GM. And they said, 'We're probably going to have to send you back down because we think you need more seasoning.' I was only like four years out of high school. I graduated in '69."

Reitz got a temporary reprieve, though. The California native would be allowed to stick around to play at home.

"They wanted to let me play in my hometown of San Francisco before they sent me out," Reitz says.

By the time the team got to San Francisco—the third city on the trip—Reitz's role with the club had dwindled. He had gone from starting nearly every game in the first three weeks to a platoon job. Often, when a right-handed pitcher started for the opposition, Reitz would sit out the start of the game. Tim McCarver, the lefty-hitting catcher, started behind the plate against righties, while Joe Torre got the call at third and Ted Simmons played first. When it was a left-hander for the other club, McCarver sat down, Simmons caught, Torre moved to first, and Reitz got his shot.

He came off the bench for three straight games early in the trip, still playing exemplary defense but holding no illusions about his status with the big league club. The Tulsa Oilers had a spot waiting for a good-field, no-hit hot-corner man.

"They needed a little more offense, and they just thought I came up early and needed a little more experience in the minor leagues, more at-bats," he says. "Plus, being platooned, you're not getting the at-bats you need to really compete at the major league level. They wanted me to play every day."

Reitz didn't like it, but he understood. He knew he wasn't lighting it up. As the trip went on, though, he showed little signs of life, even as the team struggled on. In an 11-3 loss at Dodger Stadium, Reitz went 1-for-3 with a double, a run scored, and a sacrifice fly for an RBI. And in the May 8 series opener against the Giants at Candlestick Park, he singled home a run and scored.

He was still hitting .177, but the little flashes of light gave him badly needed encouragement. Reitz kept reminding himself he could do it, and fortunately he had proved that to himself and to the team a year earlier.

Ken Reitz was known as the "Zamboni" for his stellar glovework, but he also had to show that he could hit in order to stay in the big leagues.

Brace Photos

"What helped me to even get the chance was the month I had the prior year when I came up," Reitz acknowledges. "I did so well that last month, I hit .359 in 28 games. So they knew I had the ability to hit in the major leagues. I was struggling, but I knew that at some point in time if I could turn it around, I would probably be OK."

When the Cardinals played their second of three games at Candlestick, on May 9, it wasn't just Reitz who needed a pick me up. St. Louis had lost four straight and was a dismal 5-20 on the year. The proud Cardinals had already fallen nine full games behind the hated rival Cubs in the National League East Division. The Redbirds were in dead last—a position that never, ever sits well by the banks of the Mississippi.

They had lost the day before despite sending two-time Cy Young winner Bob Gibson to the mound. In a rare struggle, Gibson gave up four home runs in the series opener, and the Cards lost, 9-7, to the West-leading Giants. In fact, it was fortunate that the Cards were in the East, rather than the western division with the Giants. Had they been in San Francisco's division, they'd have already been trailing by a gaping 14 ½ games.

Oh, and not that they needed any further obstacles, but the Giants sent a formidable hurler to the mound on that spring night by the Bay. Left-hander Ron Bryant brought a skimpy 1.82 ERA into the game. Bryant went on to lead the National League in wins that year with 24. He finished third in Cy Young balloting and was named the *Sporting News* National League Pitcher of the Year.

A day after losing with their ace, the Cards had to try to beat the other guys' ace. On some level, though, it hardly mattered to Reitz. Win or lose, stay or go, he was fulfilling a dream that week. The San Francisco kid was playing at the ballpark where he watched games as a boy. He was playing against the guys he grew up idolizing.

"It was fun for me, because I grew up about a mile away," Reitz says. "So I got to visit with family and friends. It was always cold out there, but it had a different meaning for me because I grew up watching the Giants ever since I was a little kid. I'd never left San Francisco. I grew up in the same house, and I never left until I signed with the Cardinals. I could see the lights of Candlestick Park from my bedroom. So going in to play the Giants had great meaning for me—playing against McCovey and all the great players. These were guys I grew up idolizing."

Reitz even wore No. 44 in honor of the intimidating McCovey, though he had to wait until his first full year before he could be issued the number. Someone else had it the season before. And the only thing as sweet for Reitz as playing against the Giants was playing for the Cardinals. In the pre-ESPN, pre-Internet days of the 1960s, one of the few ways to see Major League Baseball on television was to watch the World Series. So for a baseball fan born in 1951, the Cardinals World Series heroes of the 1960s played ball on a pedestal. Now Reitz was playing in the same clubhouse with them—Lou Brock, Gibson, McCarver.

"At first it was scary, because these guys were bigger than life to me," he says. "And once I got to know them, they really looked after me. Joe Torre, Lou Brock—Lou would always help me. He would always have something to say. He'd walk by, say, 'Relax, kid, just go out there and play your game.' Things like that. Same with Torre. Torre would always have the right thing to say. He knew I had the ability to be there. He just wanted me to relax and not try so hard, because that's when you put yourself in a position to slump.

"Those guys were always very encouraging. Always telling you, you're here for a reason, because you're a good player. Just hang in there and keep doing what you're doing, and stuff is going to start falling your way."

On May 9, they were proven right. Reitz was batting fifth, an expression of confidence from Schoendienst to start with. Reggie Cleveland was on the mound for St. Louis against Bryant in front of an extremely sparse officially announced crowd of 3,655. The Cardinals took a quick early lead, 1-0, thanks to a manufactured run. Brock walked, stole second, moved to third on a sacrifice, and scored when Torre grounded out. After Simmons singled, Reitz flied out to end the inning.

A pitchers' duel took shape from there, with the hurlers swapping zeroes through the fifth. Reitz flied out to right again in the fourth to fall to 0-for-2. But with none of his teammates mustering much of anything off of Bryant, it's not like he was alone in his scuffling. Torre flied out to open the sixth. Simmons grounded to first base, but a McCovey error allowed him to reach, bringing up Reitz with one out.

"I had a 3-0 count on me," Reitz recalls, "and Red let me hit away. And I swung and hit my first home run."

That is, the first home run of his entire big-league career. In a tight game, in his hometown, against a 24-game winner, and in one of the toughest hitting parks in baseball, Reitz connected. His two-run shot stretched the Cardinals lead and proved to be the decisive runs when St. Louis held on to beat San Francisco, 3-1.

"It was a high fastball, about thigh-high, and I knew it was gone as soon as I hit it," he says. "I just had that feeling. Sometimes you know."

The long ball was well received by the Reitz cheering section, which surely made up a significant percentage of the small crowd. Friends and family went wild—some a little too wild.

"It was so cool because it was at Candlestick," he says. "So my parents and probably 40 guys from my high school were there. I probably had 100 friends and family there. The guy that coached me in Little League baseball, he was kind of like the Bad News Bears— he always drank, and he owned a bar up on the corner. He had a few that day, and he wanted to come out to home plate to greet me when I got there. And I remember security grabbing him and taking him out of there."

It seems there couldn't have been many Giants fans in the park at all, in fact, because the home run ball landed in the hands of a St. Louis partisan out in the outfield seats.

"Lou Brock's niece was in left field, in the bleachers out there, and ended up with the baseball," Reitz recalls. "She was in the aisle seat, and she was running trying to get the ball. It bounced right by her and she picked it up and gave the ball to Lou, and he gave it to me after the game."

With the ball, Brock also gave his teammate some kudos. But in typical clubhouse fashion, the huzzahs were mixed with some ribbing as well.

"They all congratulated me, but it was nothing extraordinary," Reitz says. "We had a lot of veterans on the team, like Gibson and Brock and people like that, and they just said, 'It's about time you did something.'"

Yet with the homer, Reitz wasn't even done for the game. He got another at-bat and ripped a leadoff double in the ninth. Though he was stranded, it added up to his best day thus far that season. His six total bases equaled what he'd managed in his previous 11 games. His average was now pushing .200.

It was always good to be home, but going home that night for Reitz was better than ever. He swelled with pride when he went to his old house for the evening.

"I got home that night," he says, "and my dad, he was kind of a tough guy, worked for Pabst Blue Ribbon delivering beer to bars, and it was the first time I ever saw him smile at me. That was something really neat. Confidence is everything in hitting. If you get on a little roll and you start getting a few hits, you start seeing the ball better. You walk up to the plate feeling like, 'I'm going to get a base hit.' When you're in a slump, you walk up to the plate and you know you're not going to get a hit. Sometimes you just need a little kick in the butt."

Reitz picked up another base hit the next day, this one off six-time All-Star "Sudden" Sam McDowell. He stroked two doubles on the first day of the ensuing homestand, and another the day after that, adding up to a 7-for-20 stretch. By the end of May, his average was securely above .200. His slugging percentage, still not dazzling, had at least reached the mid-.300s.

"I was playing good defense, but I was struggling with the bat," he says. "I had another hit in that game, and the home run. Then the next day I had a good day, and I just got on a roll. I think I ended up . . . I can't remember what I hit for the year, but it was pretty good back then because you faced really good pitching. And I never went back to the minor leagues. That was probably the one at-bat that turned my whole career around."

Reitz never doubted he had the ability to succeed. He never felt he couldn't make it. It was simply that the reality of his situation was becoming weightier and weightier as his substandard sophomore season wore on.

He needed a spark and he got one. The same could be said for the Cardinals, who soon began their own climb from the depths of the standings. They bottomed out shortly after the road trip, then began digging their way out of the cellar. On June 23, they reached .500, and by the first week in July, they got their heads above water at 39-38. Reitz hit .321 over one particularly torrid stretch for the club, as they went 16-6 over a three-week span in late June and early July.

St. Louis even took the division lead in late July, holding first place into September. The Cards finished a game back in second place with an 81-81 record, but the rebound from their awful start was a victory in itself—much as it was for Reitz individually.

"I just needed a break, and my break came with that one pitch," he says. "That one pitch just turns your whole season around. It could be a bloop hit with the bases loaded, but mine just happened to be a game-winning homer."

It turns out that Reitz's homer in San Francisco would mark one of the few times in his career that he made headlines with his bat. He was a capable hitter but not a spectacular one, a lifetime .260 hitter with a .290 on-base percentage and .359 slugging percentage. He hit 68 home runs, 17 of them in 1977. Reitz did drive in at least 50 runs in seven straight seasons. But he was known in St. Louis not for his bat, but for his defense. His 1975 Gold Glove is his best-known award.

And then there's the nickname, which may be the way he's most remembered, and which came courtesy of broadcaster Mike Shannon.

"It was probably about '77, somewhere in there," Reitz says. "The clubhouse guys, they'd listen to the game while they were working. I came in, and one of the clubhouse kids said, 'Hey, you've got a new nickname—Zamboni. Shannon is calling you that.'

"I said, 'Why is that?' He said, 'You suck ground balls up like the Zamboni sucks the water off the field.'"

The Cardinals actually employed a Zamboni machine like the ones used at hockey arenas. It sucked the water off of the hard artificial turf and sprayed it towards the drains, aiding the drying of the field after a rain.

Had Reitz been called "Reitzie" or "KR" or "Bubba," he might not be so well-remembered today. But once he got the nickname, he had even more of a place in Cardinals lore than he already did. He's still popular, whether it be at the ballpark or out in public. He lives in the St. Louis area and can frequently be seen at new Busch Stadium.

"I think when Mike Shannon gave me that nickname, that's really what [got me noticed]. Because to this day, I'll go down there and people will yell, 'Zamboni!' It happens all the time. I just think that's the coolest nickname you could have."

Reitz didn't get to finish his career in St. Louis. He was traded in the deal that sent Bruce Sutter from the Cubs to the Cardinals. After one season as a Cub, he was released, and he added a seven-game coda to his big-league career with the Pirates in 1982.

But there's no denying where his heart is. He didn't leave it in a certain city out west; it's very much with him in the Midwest. When Reitz talks about his own career, he frequently references the modern-day Cardinals, and especially the 2006 World Series championship team. He missed out on postseason glory as a player, but he took plenty of joy when the newest batch of Redbirds won it all.

"I just think the fans are always on your side," he says. "They appreciated me because I always gave 100 percent. I never missed games. I did the little things to help us win. If we needed to move the runner over, I hit the ball the other way. I was always very high-strung and competitive. And I showed a lot of emotion, but in a good way to try to win games."

CHAPTER 18

DANNY COX

Shortly before his major league debut, Danny Cox pitched in baseball's annual exhibition in Cooperstown—the Hall of Fame game. He jokes that because he was the winner of that game, he's in the Hall of Fame.

Five days after triumphing at the Hall, though, Cox one-upped himself. He pitched brilliantly against a team that featured three Cooperstown-bound players in its starting lineup, and one more who would be there if it were simply a matter of on-field performance. That performance, Cox's big-league debut, capped a drastic rise through the ranks and an exponential increase in the quality of competition for Cox in 1983. In four months he went from pitching in games where they don't even officially keep stats to shutting out the eventual National League champions for 10 innings.

He never stopped to think about how high he'd risen, and how quickly, which is a big part of how he kept doing it. Drafted out of Troy State University in 1981, Cox began his minor league career on the typical path. He played rookie ball in the Appalachian League in '81, impressing the big club with a 9-4 record, a 2.06 ERA and 10 complete games in 13 starts.

Cox began his first full year in similar fashion after climbing one step up the ladder to full-season low Class A Springfield of the Midwest League. He put up a fine 2.56 ERA, but he sustained an arm injury and made only 13 starts. Thus sidetracked, Cox found himself a long, long way away from the big leagues at the start of 1983. He began the year in extended spring training, which is just about as far from the show as you can get. Extended spring games are watched by the teams, and they matter to the players, but for the most part, you can't even find stats for them. It's for injured players and for players who aren't ready to tackle full-season ball yet.

When he got healthy, Cox was assigned to head up one notch from where he had been the year before, to St. Petersburg of the high Class A Florida State League. He was back on schedule, but a realistic timetable still would have put him a good two years away from the majors. Instead, he compressed two years into a few months.

Cox made five starts for St. Pete before he was promoted to Double-A Arkansas of the Texas League. And as a Traveler, Cox made a striking impression. He repeated his iron-man act from rookie ball, completing seven of 11 starts at Arkansas. Cox went 8-3 with a 2.29 ERA, placing himself very much on the Cardinals' radar.

"It didn't matter where I was at," he says. "Each level you moved up, you got better so you had to play. All I thought about was getting in there and throwing strikes and pitching like what it took to get me there."

Cox was named a Double-A all-star, but barely hung around long enough to enjoy the honor. After 11 starts he was on his way up to Triple-A Louisville, and he was clearly in St. Louis' plans. He made all of two starts for Louisville, not getting a decision, before he made a stop that was sort of halfway in between the minors and the majors. Cox was summoned to start for St. Louis in the Hall of Fame Game against Baltimore.

Cox held the O's to a run on six innings, unfazed by a tough opponent. Baltimore won the World Series that year behind a lineup that featured future Hall of Famers Cal Ripken Jr. (named the American League MVP for '83) and Eddie Murray.

It wasn't the competition that jarred Cox. It was the surroundings. His whirlwind had taken him all over the map, but big-league mores were still foreign to him. After all, he'd never even been in major league Spring Training.

As a kid pitcher facing a team full of Hall of Fame-caliber players, Danny Cox held his own and earned his team's trust and respect. *Brace Photos*

"I went there, and I didn't really know what to expect," he says. "I didn't know what that was about. I threw on the side, on flat ground. There was no mound. It's old-school baseball. I got the win, so I always tell people I'm in the Hall of Fame, because I won the Hall of Fame game in '83. I got on the bus in Cooperstown and sat in the front seat, and one of the guys said, 'You can't sit there. That's where the skipper sits.' Well, I definitely ain't going to the back. You have to have some [service] time to do that. They gave me a hard time about that, but I didn't know."

Whatever faux pas Cox may have committed, it was surely not enough to deter his march to the big leagues. The Hall of Fame game was a pitching test, and he passed. Later in the week, he was formally notified that he was St. Louis-bound. Cox drove from Louisville to St. Louis on Friday, August 5, knowing he'd face the potent Phillies the next day. He'd been prepared not only by his pitching experiences, but by his coaches and the organization. Cox learned the Cardinal way of doing things in the minors, so he was ready not only in terms of talent but in terms of approach.

"Respect for the game," he says. "That's what I was taught, is respect for the game. No matter what position you're in, you play that game as hard as you can.

"If you give as much as you have, you're going to get that in return. And I think that was a Cardinal tradition. Be on time, be ready to play, do everything to prepare yourself before the game starts, run out every ball."

Even so, Cox's first assignment was tailor-made to spook a kid pitcher. The Phils were battling the Pirates atop the National League East, and their lineup was dotted with the kinds of names that make pitchers' knees go weak. Batting second was Pete Rose, closing in on 4,000 hits and at that time seemingly a Cooperstown lock. In the three spot, Joe Morgan, having a tough year but arguably the greatest second baseman since World War II. Hitting cleanup was the still very much in his prime Mike Schmidt, another immortal who finished the '83 season with 40 home runs. Oh, and in the nine spot? That would be still another Hall of Famer-to-be, left-hander Steve Carlton.

A starting pitcher will always repeat the mantra that he's not pitching against the other pitcher. He's pitching against the opposing lineup. That's tougher when you're making your debut and the other guy has 295 victories.

"I knew who he was, and that he was a future Hall of Famer," Cox says. "Without a doubt, I knew that. But then, I was pitching against other future Hall of Famers too. I didn't overwhelm myself with that, because I was already overwhelmed being there to begin with. This team brought me up to pitch today. So that's why I'm here."

He got some reassurance right away.

"I can remember Greg Gross was the first guy that I faced," he says. "I threw him two fastballs and a breaking ball, all three strikes, he took them all and he sat down. I thought, 'What the heck did I just do? I actually threw three strikes in a row.'"

And then just as quickly, he was in trouble. Rose singled and Morgan doubled, putting runners on second and third for Schmidt. In a lineup full of vaunted hitters, none was scarier than Schmidt. Yet Cox escaped, getting Schmidt and Joe Lefebvre to line out and end the inning. He had survived his first jam, and he took a breath.

"I didn't want to walk everybody," Cox said, recalling coming right at Schmidt. "I had been pitching well that year. I went all the way from extended spring to the big leagues. This is what you've been playing for."

Cox rolled through a 1-2-3 second inning, inducing a groundball out from Von Hayes before striking out Bo Diaz and Ivan DeJesus. He repeated the feat in the third, as Carlton struck out and Gross and Rose both grounded out. With two outs in the bottom of the third, it was time for Cox's first at-bat, something that had him as flummoxed as anything about the entire day.

"I've been in the minor leagues for a couple years, and now I've got to take BP," he says. "I haven't taken BP all year. 'Get a few bunts down, do this, do that.' It was all new. I wasn't used to getting to the ballpark and getting batting gloves and a bat."

To top it off, he was swinging against Carlton.

"One of the biggest things was my first at-bat," he says. "I flied out to right field, and I was about as happy as you could be. F9! Somebody said to me, 'What are you smiling at?' I said, 'Hey, I hit it!' I hadn't hit in four years."

In the fourth, Cox got in another jam. He got Morgan to strike out looking, and Schmidt grounded out, but Lefebvre drew Cox's first walk of the game. Hayes singled, putting men on first and second, but Diaz struck out.

He wasn't getting in much trouble, but when he did, Cox was able to get out. He was in command even if he wasn't dominating. As far removed as the Phillies were from extended spring training, he viewed it as simply an extension of what he had been doing for four months.

"I wasn't really thinking about that feeling," he said. "I was just pitching. I had been pitching well all year. So I was on a roll. I was just pitching well. And that's all I was thinking about. It wasn't like, 'Today, all my stuff is there.' It was there to begin with. It was a continuation. No matter who I was pitching against, it was me."

The Cardinals loaded the bases with two outs in the bottom of the fourth, but failed to score. In the fifth, Cox found himself in still another pickle. After DeJesus grounded out, Carlton laced a double. Gross' groundout advanced Carlton to third, and manager Whitey Herzog had a decision. He put it in his rookie pitcher's hands.

"Whitey came out because there were two outs and a man on third, and Rose was coming up," Cox relates. "He asks me, 'Do you want to pitch to Rose? Or do you want to walk him and pitch to Morgan?' and I said, 'I'll be honest with you, Whitey. Morgan has been swinging real good at me. He seems to see the ball real good off me. He's got a double. He's hit the ball hard. I'd rather pitch to Rose.' He said, 'You know he's got like 4,000 hits, don't you?' I said, 'Yeah.'

"He goes, 'OK' and walks off. I didn't want to walk somebody to pitch to somebody else at that time. I didn't want to do that anyway. I'm pitching well. I'm going to come after you."

Cox's gut didn't lead him astray. Rose grounded out to third base, and the runner was stranded.

Unfortunately, Carlton continued to toy with the Redbirds. Another 1-2-3 in the fifth kept it a 0-0 game. Cox didn't get the bat on the ball this time, striking out against "Lefty." Cox dodged danger in a strange sixth. Morgan walked and stole second, but was thrown out at third when Schmidt grounded into a fielder's choice. Schmidt, meanwhile, took off with one out, and when Lefebvre lined to left field, the slugger was gunned down before he could get back to first base.

"There was always somebody on," Cox recalls. "It was always a situation where they had a chance to score."

Carlton worked out of a first-and-third, two-out situation in the sixth, and Cox stranded more runners in the seventh. Hayes singled and moved to second on a sacrifice with one out. But Cox coaxed groundouts from DeJesus and Carlton, and the scoreless tie rolled on.

"At that time, I was throwing the ball well, and I was confident," he says. "I was being aggressive. I knew they were a good team. This was August, and they were a first-place team. But I just went after them."

Cox batted with a runner on base in the seventh, a pretty good indicator that Herzog and pitching coach Hub Kittle were enamored of his performance. He finally got to enjoy a 1-2-3 inning in the eighth, but he still didn't have any runs to work with. The Cardinals put two runners on base with two outs in the bottom of the eighth, but again couldn't convert. So Cox and the Cards went to the ninth. He got Schmidt yet again, this time on a fly to right. Lefebvre singled and Hayes struck out. Facing Diaz, Cox recorded strikeout No. 8. And if he'd gotten even one run, he would already have been done for the day with a shutout win. The fans wanted to give him a curtain call, but his veteran teammates were having none of it. And neither was Cox.

"I remember throwing a slider that I left up and in, but he swung through it," Cox says. "After the ninth, I go in the dugout, and they all start standing up. The fans give me a standing O. I was sitting there, and I'm not done pitching yet. I haven't accomplished anything. And I remember Dave LaPoint saying, 'Don't you go out there, man.' I said, 'I'm not going out there. I'm still pitching.'"

Never mind that he had started the year in A ball. The kid had an idea about the rules of the road, despite the fact that it was his first game. DeJesus and pinch hitter Tony Perez grounded out to open the 10th, with Perez hitting for Carlton. If nothing else, Cox had at least outlasted the Hall of Famer, one feather in his cap already. Gross singled, but Rose flied out to end the 10th. Now Cox could acknowledge the fans.

"I got out of that and came back in the dugout," he says. "And Whitey says, 'That's good.' I looked around, and LaPoint goes, 'Go out there now!' So I went out and tipped my hat and came back in."

Cox was removed for a pinch hitter in the bottom of the 10th, but the Cardinals again could not score—this time against reliever Al Holland. After a night of hard work during the summer in St. Louis, Cox ducked into the clubhouse to change out of his sweaty jersey. It was then that he realized how much his stock had soared in the organization. A call from the owner will do that.

"As I was in there changing my shirt, Buddy Bates, the equipment manager, comes over and says, 'Coxie, Mr. [Gussie] Busch is on the phone.' And I thought, being a rookie, he was just pulling my leg. I said, 'No, no, no, no, you're not getting me.' He goes, 'Coxie, I swear to God.' He was nervous and all that. And I said, 'No, man, you're not getting me.' He says, 'Coxie, I swear to God, you've got to answer the phone. He's waiting.' And I said, 'All right.' So I went.

"'Hello?' 'Hello? Is this Danny Cox?' 'Yes sir, it is.' He goes, 'Great game tonight.' I said, 'Well, thank you very much sir.' Now, the game is still going on. And he goes, 'Well, I hope you're here for a long, long time.' I said, 'Well, I guess that's up to you, isn't it, sir?'

"And he goes, 'Ha ha ha, you're right, it is. Bye.'"

At 84 years old, and with 30 years' service as the owner of the Cardinals, Busch was the father of the franchise at that time. According to Cox, Bates told him that it was the first time Busch had ever called the clubhouse to speak with a player.

And the accolades were just beginning. After removing Cox, meanwhile, Herzog did the only logical thing. He turned to his relief ace, Bruce Sutter, for the 11th. Sutter couldn't hold the fort, though. Morgan cracked a leadoff double, took third on a Schmidt fly ball out and scored two batters after that when Hayes singled. The Cardinals couldn't respond in the bottom of the 11th. After all his work, Cox didn't have a win. He didn't have a complete game or a shutout. He had some memories, and he had plenty of phone calls and pats on the back.

"Whitey came up to me after the game, and he said, 'Usually, when you pitch 10 shutout innings, you get a win.' I said, 'Well, it's a tough league. That's the way it goes.' Sutter came up to me and said, 'Hey man, sorry about that.' And I said, 'I know you're going to save a lot more for me.'"

Even the opponents took notice. One of Cox's favorite players, and one of the game's great competitors, sought him out later.

"The next day, I was down the right-field line and I see Pete Rose walk across to me," Cox recalls, with excitement even 24 years later. "And he goes, 'Great game last night.' I said thank you, and he goes, 'Keep pitching like that and you'll be around a long time.' I said, 'Thanks man,' and he just turned around and walked off.

"Third day in the big leagues, for somebody to come up and say that to you. And I always watched Pete Rose when I was growing up. I thought he was the epitome of a baseball player. Charlie Hustle, he earned that."

After handling himself on the field, Cox was showing that he also had a clue about conducting himself in a big-league clubhouse. He didn't show anyone up or show his frustration. But neither did he commit the mortal sin of reveling in individual accomplishment after a team loss.

"I think that situation built a lot of relationships for me in baseball," he says. "It showed that I did care. I wasn't just going through the motions."

Moreover, his showing in the game had bolstered the regard that the organization already had for him. It didn't cement his place in the majors permanently, but he showed quite a bit. He showed he wouldn't scare in a big situation, and he showed he could go deep into games.

"Whitey knew I could pitch a complete game," he says. "So as far as that goes, I think it probably helped to know that I could go that long. It gave me confidence in the late innings. That was always important. If it's 1-1, you're still going out there. You may have to hit in the seventh."

Cox spent the remainder of '83 in the Cardinals' starting rotation, though his debut was a portent of his luck for the rest of the season. He was drilled in his next start, but in his third big-league game he was once again deprived of a deserved win. Cox went seven innings against the Expos, allowing three runs, but got no decision in a Cards victory. Finally he got a win in his fourth start—a home game against the Astros. Two weeks after matching up with Carlton, he received another intimidating task: going up against Nolan Ryan. This time, not only did he pitch well, he was credited with the victory and picked up his first major league base hit.

For much of the rest of the year, Cox didn't get the wins to reflect how well he was throwing. He allowed one earned run in 6⅓ innings in a loss to Houston. He pitched nine innings, allowing two runs, but St. Louis lost in 10 innings to the Reds. In his season finale, Cox gave up two earned runs to the Expos in 6⅔ innings, but was the losing pitcher in a 4-0 defeat.

The '84 season started poorly for Cox, and in June he was sent back to Louisville. But after a five-week retooling in the minors, he returned to the bigs to stay. Cox finished solid in '84, going 6-3 with a 3.72 ERA after his recall. By '85 he was a central piece on a championship team, winning 18 games as the Cards made the World Series for the second time in four years. And in '87 he enjoyed the game that most fans think of first when they think of Cox.

Matching up with Atlee Hammaker, Cox pitched an eight-hit, no-walk shutout in Game 7 of the 1987 NLCS. He pushed the Redbirds back to the World Series once again. He cherishes that game, but in a sense it's just a game for him. His debut was an experience in a way that no subsequent game could match.

"Those kinds of other things, that's why you talk about [it as] the most memorable," he says. "It's not just the game, it's everything else with that combined."

Cox, like so many of his contemporaries, remained in the St. Louis area after his career was over—even though he didn't finish his career as a Cardinal. He managed the Gateway Grizzlies in the independent Frontier League, and makes a point of getting back to Busch Stadium when he can. He tries to pass along to the current players what was always passed along to him by veterans and his predecessors.

"The Yankees, the Dodgers, whatever traditions they have, which are quite extensive, it's nothing more than the Cardinals," he says. "I guarantee you. There's absolutely nothing more than the Cardinals, wherever you go. That's a tradition passed down. Guys before me were kicking ass. I kicked ass when I was playing. I want to see you kick ass. There's no jealousy involved in it. That's what makes it fun."

CHAPTER 19

MIKE SHANNON

To sit down and talk baseball with Mike Shannon is to know that you're going to be around for a while. And regardless of what you start asking about, you know you'll have covered a whole lot of ground by the time you're done. Asking Shannon to single out a memorable game from his playing career does, in fact, yield an answer, but not an obvious one. He points to playing behind Ray Washburn when Washburn no-hit the Giants on September 18, 1968. But it's not a conversation about Washburn pitching and Willie Mays at the plate and Shannon at third base for very long.

It veers. The discussion touches on the differences between the '67 and '68 Cardinals as opposed to the '64 ballclub; the comparison between those teams and the 2004-2005 Redbirds; playing behind Bob Gibson; the relative merits of Babe Ruth versus modern-day players; the sanctity of the game's records, and so much more. This is simply how it is when you begin to pick the baseball brain of a man who has been affiliated with one of the game's great franchises for 50 years. Not to mention someone whose job description is all about telling stories.

"You have to have a respect and reverence for the game," Shannon says. "I do, anyway. This game is so honored in our country. The records are so honored. You can see what it means now, because we've had the steroids situation. Whoa, this is the holy grail you're talking about. This is something you don't tread on. That's really what we're talking about. Don't be messing with it."

Shannon enjoyed a successful playing career, albeit a brief one. He signed with the Cardinals organization in 1958, and reached the majors in '62. He was a close to a full-timer by '64. Illness ended his playing days in 1970, when he was 31, but Shannon is a Cardinal for life. So he moved straight into the front office in '71, and in '72 he joined Jack Buck in the broadcast booth. He has stayed there, through several partners and a series of highs and lows for the team.

"You have to report the game," he says. "But if you're going to be on there for three, 3 ½ hours, you've got to be a little entertaining too. This is a game, but this is entertainment. Somebody's got that radio on for three, 3 ½ hours, they get tired of ball, strike, ball, strike. And sometimes they get tired of the game. If you get a bad game, you better start talking about something else."

The 2007 season marked Shannon's 50th year in the organization, from minor league player to voice of the ballclub. At the end of the season, the team commemorated his 50 years with an on-field ceremony and plenty of tributes. He has become one of the true faces of the organization and one of its best-known personalities. Certainly, no one has a better idea of what the "Birds on the Bat" really mean than the man who has represented them in six decades.

"It is both on and off the field," he says. "You are representing not only the organization, but you are also representing the city of St. Louis and the fans. And I think the fans have a lot to do with it. The fans take such great pride in their baseball team. And make no mistake, it's their team. It's not the players' team. It's not the owners' team. It's the fans' team. Ownership, they're really just the custodians of it."

And it's Shannon, more than anyone, who keeps the fans connected to their team. So it makes sense that from a life as a Cardinal, Shannon doesn't have just one or two memories. He doesn't hang his hat on one or two games or plays. And the ones that do stand out are not the same as the ones many fans think of. Shannon the man, not to mention Shannon the broadcaster, is an amalgam of all of his experiences, all the miles he's traveled, all the pitches he's seen, swung at,

---

'Mike Shannon's playing career was cut short, but 40 years later, he's become a Cardinals icon thanks to his work in the broadcast booth. *Brace Photos*

and called, all the clubhouses and radio booths he's called home. He believes he's still getting better.

"I'm a guy that doesn't look back," he says. "I've had to because of the situation, the ballclub coming to me and asking me about honoring me. But I'm not a guy that looks back. Somebody asks me, name one game. Well, the game is the game tonight. And I really mean that."

Many of Shannon's contemporaries are gone in one way or another. Buck, his longtime partner, passed away in 2002. Teammates like Bob Gibson and Lou Brock are certainly visible, but they're not part of the daily life of the team like Shannon is. Red Schoendienst, one of the few men with more years as a Cardinal than Shannon, is still around, but his role is not as public. Stan Musial, the greatest Cardinal of them all, has grown ill and frail and makes few appearances.

Shannon stands in many respects as the dean of Cardinals baseball and the face of the franchise in the community. His pride in the organization is intense, and it's that pride that defines his favorite day wearing the "Birds on the Bat" on his chest. Shannon played in three World Series, two on the winning end. But for Shannon, the day that sums up what it meant to play Cardinals baseball was actually a meaningless game in the standings. It's the way his teammates handled the game that said it all.

On Sunday, September 15, 1968, Steve Carlton pitched a complete game and Roger Maris hit a three-run homer, securing the Cardinals' third pennant in five seasons. Curt Flood had five hits in the 7-4 win over Houston at the Astrodome. For the next two weeks, the team's only responsibilities were to show up, stay healthy and not embarrass themselves. The games counted for nothing.

And so the Cardinals, as newly crowned National League champions, celebrated. They celebrated in Houston on Sunday afternoon. Then they got on a plane for their next series, in San Francisco. They celebrated on the plane, and they celebrated when they landed in California. This is what major league teams do when they win a title. You put in seven months of hard work, every day. And when you achieve what you've been pushing so hard for, you let loose.

It was particularly true in the Cardinals' case, because they had 11 more games before the World Series. It would be quite some time before they played another meaningful game. They even had an off day in between the Sunday clincher and the Tuesday series opener at Candlestick Park. They had plenty of reason and plenty of time to enjoy themselves—and plenty of time to sleep in afterward. And so they did. Unfortunately, when they got to San Francisco, they celebrated a little too publicly, and it caught the eye of a local reporter. Their Monday night festivities were captured in photographs and print.

"We go out to this restaurant/bar kind of deal and had another celebration out there," Shannon recalls. "So the next morning I got up and on that newspaper, in big block letters, it said, 'Wine, Women, Song.' It was a public place! There were all kinds of people there! Everybody was celebrating. I read this thing, and it's all about how we partied. And the last paragraph said, 'If they make it to the ballpark tonight, Gaylord Perry will probably no-hit them.'"

Rarely, if ever has a baseball scribe been so correct with such a bold prediction. Or even a timid one. With little reason to get up for the game, the Cardinals turned in far from their best effort. A number of regulars rested, as is custom after a clinching game.

The combination allowed the Hall of Fame-bound Perry to no-hit the Cardinals. Bob Gibson pitched brilliantly in the midst of his historic Cy Young season, striking out 10 in a four-hit complete game, but lost 1-0. The game was over in a brisk one hour and 40 minutes. The Cardinals were peeved, to put it gently. Shannon put it more coarsely. Their pride had been assaulted, and that was a dangerous thing to do to a team so good.

"The next day we had a day game at noon," Shannon says, "and Ray Washburn no-hit them! It's the first time in the history of the game that there were back-to-back no-hitters. And it happened in less than 24 hours. It looked like we read the paper and said, 'Well, OK, that old so-and-so, we'll just go ahead and let Gaylord no-hit us, and then we'll no-hit them.' And that team was about that good to be able to do that, too. That's the happiest I think I've ever been about a ballgame."

The bats didn't immediately come to life for the Cardinals, though. For six innings, Washburn hadn't allowed a hit but still didn't have a lead. In the seventh, Shannon doubled home Orlando Cepeda for the winning run. The Cardinals added one more, but

Shannon was already looking ahead to helping to preserve his teammate's moment.

"Once you get past the sixth inning you start thinking about it," Shannon explains. "You're very cognizant of it after five innings. In the sixth inning you pay attention. And in the seventh, it's all over but the shouting. You're six outs away. Every pitch just becomes—you're thinking about every pitch anyway, but when you have that, it's all magnified. It's right there. It's the boiling point."

As the ninth drew closer, Shannon did more and more thinking ahead. He pieced through the lineup, figuring out who would come up when. And he realized that he likely would face one more serious test before the game was over. Willie Mays was 37 and on the tail end of his career, but still dangerous and still frightening. Shannon didn't want to be the person who failed to make a play and cost Washburn his no-hitter.

"I knew he was coming up in the ninth inning," says Shannon. "And Mays, if he hits the ball on the ground, he only hits it to the left side. So I'm thinking, 'OK . . .' I'm thinking this in the seventh inning, and I know I'm thinking it in the eighth. I know he's coming up. And I'm thinking, 'I've got to touch it somehow.'

"When he hit it on the ground, he just got on top. And he was pulling it, so he smoked it. So anyway, sure as heck, he comes up and it's bang-bang. And I catch it. Well, I forgot all about throwing the damn thing! But I threw a sinker over, Cepeda sucked it up and we had the no-hitter."

As a result, the Cardinals enjoyed one more raucous celebration. This one may have been tinged with a little more spite than the unbridled glee of the pennant party. It was plenty sweet either way.

"That's the happiest I've ever been in the game, just because of that article, a guy trying to capitalize and sensationalize," Shannon says.

Without similar motivations, the Cardinals lost their next five games before rebounding to take three of the final four before the World Series. But they showed what they were capable of doing. They showed what happened if you poked the sleeping beast.

"We had just won the pennant," Shannon says of Perry's no-hit game. "Who's going to play? That's really the attitude. And we had about two weeks to go anyway, so nobody was really giving a damn.

But when he did no-hit us, that pissed us off and we said, 'We'll show them.' It was just an unbelievable circumstance how that all happened. That team, if there was ever a team that could pull something off like that, it was that team."

And from there, Shannon begins to recall the other great teams he was a part of. The Cardinals of the mid-to-late 1960s were the dominant franchise in baseball, with three pennants and two world titles. But the '64 team had a bit of a different cast from the '67 and '68 clubs.

The '64 Cardinals were a mix of rising youngsters like Shannon, McCarver, Curt Flood, and Brock, along with well-established veterans such as Dick Groat, Ken Boyer, and Curt Simmons. By '68, much of the older guard had moved on, while the youngsters had taken their places as franchise centerpieces. The '64 team had to come from behind to win the pennant, and finished with 93 wins to eke out the championship. The '67 and '68 teams ran roughshod over the league, combining for 198 wins and taking the division by 10 ½ and nine games respectively.

"The '64 team I think had more stars," Shannon says. "But the '67 and '68 teams were probably as professional and as proficient as I've ever seen. We just never beat ourselves, and went about it in a methodical way. Red [Schoendienst, manager] filled out the lineup in Spring Training and went right on through the World Series. It was amazing."

The 1960s teams stand alongside a few other eras as one of the great runs in Cardinals history. They may be the most revered Cards clubs thanks to the preeminence of Gibson and Brock. Within the league, though, there was no question about their status. The Redbirds overran the National League with talent, execution, and attitude.

"I hit home runs in all three World Series I played in, hit a home run off of Whitey Ford, played for my hometown team, and all that was a big thrill," Shannon says. "But the satisfaction was just winning. It never meant anything to me otherwise. The satisfaction after you won a game, you knew you won, just to sit back and relax and enjoy that. That was the whole thrill. The satisfaction, plain and simple."

Shannon still marvels at the experience of playing alongside

Gibson, one of the great big-game pitchers ever to step on a mound. For an individual performance, he singles out Gibson's 1968 World Series performance as easily the best he ever saw from field level. Gibson allowed five hits and a walk, but he struck out 17 and simply overwhelmed the eventual world champion Tigers.

"That was one of the most amazing feats ever," Shannon insists. "That was one of the finest hitting ballclubs ever. They really were a good hitting baseball team. It wasn't that he struck out 17. It looked like a big leaguer pitching against high school guys. That's how dominant he was. I asked those guys years later—Norm Cash when he was alive, and Kaline—and they said they'd never seen anything like it.

"All I did was throw the ball around the field. I was in awe. That's the one game ever that I was just in awe of a guy. I was flabbergasted. He was so overpowering, so dominating, it was unbelievable. You go back years later and ask about it, they'd never seen anything like that. And I'd never seen anything like it."

Shannon treasures his time on the field with those great teams, but he doesn't live in the past. At the time, though, playing for the Cardinals had particular resonance for him. He was a local boy, after all. Shannon is a St. Louis native who attended Christian Brothers College High School. He played high school football with Stan Musial's son. Not only does he have 50 years as a member of the Cardinals organization—he was looking on from up close even before that. He was a teammate of Musial's for two years, learning the Cardinal way of doing things from "Stan the Man" and Boyer and other distinguished veterans.

"Those '60s clubs had a lot to do with it, but it came from guys before us also," he says. "The Kenny Boyers and the Dick Groats and the Bob Skinners and the Carl Sawatskis and Curt Simmons and Bobby Shantzes and Stan Musial. All those guys, when I came to the big leagues, were on that team. Bill White. Julian Javier. I sat there for two years and kept my mouth shut. If you opened your mouth somebody would stick a towel in it.

"To think that you had that kind of experience and that kind of quality and class. I learned from them. Those guys taught us, and then we taught the next generation. That's how you pass it on."

It was handed to the '70s clubs, even the ones that struggled. It was passed to the '80s mini-dynasty, as players like Tom Herr and

Bob Forsch kept alive the St. Louis way of doing things. It stayed alive in the lean 1990s, and certainly has been embraced by the Tony La Russa-era clubs of the late '90s and early 21st century. And one constant throughout has been Shannon. He has played in or called eight Cardinals World Series, and has been on the winning side four times.

As he looks back over the decades, more games rise to the surface. He remembers a game the Pirates' Don Robinson threw in St. Louis, not for the stats or the outcome, but because of the sheer electricity of Robinson's stuff. He recalls Mark Whiten's four-homer game. He points out that Fernando Tatis' record of two grand slams, in the same inning, off the same pitcher, may be the safest record in all of baseball. When you get Mike Shannon talking about baseball, it's going to be a long and memorable conversation. Sometimes it winds around to the micro-aspects of the game.

"There are so many different ways that you can contribute to a win," he says. "Defensively, psychologically, motivating a teammate or taking a step to the left when you've got a feeling the ball is going to be hit there. There are just so many ways that you can contribute in a baseball game without getting a hit or making a play."

It was those things that Shannon prided himself in doing as a player. He did them because it was the way he was taught. He took pride in doing it that way, just like the Cardinals before him and the Cardinals after him. He takes that pride, the pride that was instilled in him and the pride that showed up on that day in September of 1968, and applies it to his job in the booth. No one who listens to a Cardinals game would ever doubt that Shannon loves the franchise. He takes his connection with the team and its fans extremely seriously.

"It's unbelievably important," he says. "I'll run into a guy who will say, 'Hey, Mike, how you doing?' And I've never met this guy in my life. But as far as he's concerned, he knows me. He's with me every night. I understand that. I know what a tremendous responsibility that is. I just take it in every day. I'm so proud that I can be that. It's fun for me."

CHAPTER 20

CHRIS CARPENTER

Chris Carpenter became a high school star, a first-round draft pick, and a hot prospect on physical ability. He became a Cy Young winner and a World Series hero after he learned to harness that ability on every single pitch. Dating all the way back to his amateur days, Carpenter was a big guy with a big arm and big-time stuff. He made it to the majors at age 22 and won 12 games as a 23-year-old.

Though Carpenter was drafted out of high school at age 19, he still moved through the Blue Jays organization quickly, spending about 2½ seasons in the minors before reaching the Toronto. Carpenter, along with Roy Halladay and Kelvim Escobar, was vaunted as part of the forefront of a bright, bright future for the Jays.

Upon making the show, however, Carpenter finally came up against one of the most fundamental truths of playing baseball: it's very, very hard to do. He was rocked in each of his first two starts, allowing 14 runs in 5 ⅓ innings in May of 1997. He headed back to Triple-A Syracuse after three starts before making a late July return. Even then, the young man with all the physical tools scuffled. He started his career 0-5 with an 8.89 ERA before tasting success at the top level for the first time. Carpenter finished his rookie year with six straight quality starts, an indicator that maybe things were coming together.

Carpenter began to deliver on his promise in his first full season, going 12-7 with a better than average ERA for a solid, 88-win team. He was learning every day, not just every start, and how could he not?

The Toronto staff was loaded with veterans who set superb examples.

At the front of the rotation was Roger Clemens, a Hall of Fame-bound superstar still enjoying an extended career prime. Woody Williams, later Carpenter's teammate again in Toronto, took a great interest in young Carpenter, wowed by his stuff. Pat Hentgen was young at 29, but well established with a Cy Young Award and a reputation as a top-flight teammate. Even Juan Guzman set a fine example for Carpenter and his fellow youngsters, Escobar and Halladay. Carpenter watched, listened, worked—and got better. He was smart enough to realize the resources he had at his disposal, and dedicated enough to work to take advantage of it.

"I think I learned over the years that that's what you need to do to help you get better," he says. "There wasn't anybody who really said, 'Listen, you need to take something (from this).' It was just the constant experience of trying to figure out what I needed to do to get to the level that I wanted to get to. And I learned that part of it is to take everything positive, make a positive out of everything every day.

"Make sure you're working your butt off every day at whatever the task you're doing and try to learn something new every day. And it's not even just about pitching. I just listen and try to learn. Learn by watching the infield guys do their stuff, see how they do their footwork. I just try to watch and learn something different every day."

In '99, though, Carpenter endured his first bout with arm trouble—bone spurs in his pitching elbow ended his season prematurely. He struggled through a subpar 2000, but enjoyed his best season to date with a 4.09 ERA, 157 strikeouts, and 215 ⅔ innings pitched in '01. He earned the Opening Day start for Toronto in '02, and he was just starting to make a little money.

And then in the space of a year, everything turned. Carpenter endured an unsuccessful and injury-shortened '02 season, going 4-5 and pitching just 73 ⅓ innings. He underwent surgery to repair a labrum tear in his right shoulder. The Jays removed him from the 40-man roster, and Carpenter elected free agency. He signed with the Cardinals in hopes of being able to make a late-season contribution

Chris Carpenter missed out on the 2004 World Series, but when he finally did get to pitch in the Fall Classic, he made the most of the opportunity. *AP/WWP*

in '03, but suffered a setback and missed the entire season. At times he wondered whether he would be able to pitch again. It was without question the toughest period of his career.

But it was while he was out, rehabbing and missing the game desperately, that Carpenter truly became the pitcher who would dominate National League hitters for the next three seasons. Because even as Carpenter was watching his veteran teammates and trying to learn from them, he hadn't fully processed it.

When he came to camp with the Cardinals in 2004, fully healthy, Carpenter had taken enormous steps in the mental part of the game. He mastered the complete and unwavering focus that made him as dominating on a Tuesday night in May as in a playoff game in October. Carpenter learned that the secret is not in getting up for the big games. It's in never letting down in the first place.

"For me, every game that I pitch, I take the same mental approach," he says. "And that is, one pitch at a time, eliminate the outside stuff, and go out and try to execute your game plan. And then during the game, if there are certain things in the plan that aren't working, you need to adjust."

Carpenter's tunnel vision is all but unmatched by other pitchers. Now he's the veteran whom the kids watch, hoping to understand how he does what he does. He pitched under the radar in 2004, first among equals on a deep starting staff for a 105-win team. Though that pennant-winning team was advertised as having no ace, those who watched them know they had an ace, and it was Carpenter.

He reveled in pitching for a good team, loved his teammates and delighted in putting the mental and physical together. He was on his way to the first postseason of his career, and likely would have been the Game 1 starter in the playoffs—until yet another injury struck, this one truly bizarre. Carpenter sustained a nerve problem in the biceps of his pitching arm, and he was shut down for the final weeks of the season and the postseason. He missed the Division Series win over the Dodgers and the epic seven-game series against Houston.

He was a spectator when his teammates were swept in the World Series. Carpenter, who grew up in New England, missed out on playing in the Fall Classic at Fenway Park and was helpless to keep his team from being embarrassed in front of the country. And worst of all, he had no way of knowing whether he'd get another chance.

A year later, Carpenter and the Cards were teased by the thought of the World Series. They won 100 games. Carpenter stayed healthy and ultimately earned the Cy Young Award. But they were eliminated in another compelling NLCS against Houston. Once again, it was evidenced just how hard it is to win a pennant.

In 2006, the Cards almost didn't even make the postseason at all. The National League Central race came down to the season's final weekend as the Redbirds squandered a huge division advantage. Their lead over Houston slipped to as small as one half-game, and on Sunday, October 1, they were 1½ games ahead. The Astros' season ended on Sunday, but St. Louis faced the possibility of a makeup game with the Giants if they lost and the Astros won.

Manager Tony La Russa gambled that both of those things wouldn't happen, and held Carpenter out of his scheduled start. That allowed the ace to go in Game 1 of the playoffs, and it worked out perfectly. The Astros lost in Atlanta, giving the Cardinals their third straight division title and setting up Carpenter to open the playoffs.

"In '04 and '05, there's no question that our teams were [great]—we won 100-some games each year," Carpenter recalls. "We had that consistent starting pitching every time out. That year was just a battle through, and we made it. It's just weird. Leading up to the end of the season, I didn't know if I was going to pitch the last day of the season or not, and they take a shot and say, 'Screw it, we're not going to pitch you because we need you.' And then still to make it, and then the start of those playoffs, there was just a different attitude."

Though the Cardinals limped into October with 83 wins, they came alive in the postseason, and it started with Carpenter. He went 2-0 in the Division Series win over the Padres but had something of a rough NLCS. After starting Game 6 of that series, he couldn't go until Game 3 of the World Series. After the stops and starts, Carpenter's dream was in front of him.

"There's a lot of guys that play a long time and don't get an opportunity at all," Carpenter says. "For me to be able to have two opportunities—one and not be able to pitch, which I thought was going to be my only opportunity to do it—[was amazing]. A lot of things have to go right. You can ask a lot of guys. I played with a lot of veteran guys in Toronto that played a long time and never had the opportunity to do that. And I was able to do it twice. That was unbelievable. You continue to strive each year to do it, but you just never know. That made it that much more special to be able to go out and do it."

Carpenter, typically a businesslike pitcher, even enjoyed the festivities surrounding his start. He had fun with the extracurriculars. Perhaps most out of character, he says he even enjoyed his pregame news conference. But when game day came, Carpenter did what he had spent years learning to do. He truly treated it like every other day. In addition to the influence of pitchers like Clemens, Hentgen, and Williams, he also picked up a valuable mental trick from La Russa. If you treat every single game like it's the World Series, you won't freak out when the World Series comes.

Carpenter definitely didn't freak out.

"The bottom line is, you eliminate the outside stuff," Carpenter explains. "The big game, World Series game, all the people watching, it was a big game for us, but you eliminate all that and just concentrate [on the fact that] the only thing I can control is going out and making pitches. If you do that, you're going to be successful. And I was able to do it."

The series was squared at one game each after the first two games in Detroit. Anthony Reyes pitched a dazzling game in the opener, and Kenny Rogers stifled the Cardinals in Game 2. They headed back to St. Louis for a pivotal game, and both Carpenter and the Tigers entered it believing they had an advantage.

Four months earlier, Carpenter had pitched against the Tigers, and he was hit hard. In the midst of a lengthy slump for St. Louis— the kind of slump that the ace is supposed to stop—Carpenter had one of his worst games of the year. He struck out nine and didn't walk a batter, but he was roughed up for seven runs in seven innings. Detroit won the game, 10-6. If you were on the Detroit side of things, you could only view the matchup as reason for optimism. But for Carpenter, there was plenty to like as well.

"They beat me around a little bit, but I really knew that I had a good game plan that day for them," he remembers. "I just didn't execute real well. And I knew coming into that game, from watching in that series and watching them throughout the World Series that my game plan was still the right game plan. And I knew that I could execute it, and if I executed it, it would be a good game."

After Sunday night travel and Monday news conferences, Tuesday finally arrived. Carpenter, of course, was all wound up. But, he insists, no more wound up than any other start day.

"That's the thing. Every day that I pitch, I wake up and I'm nervous in the morning," he says. "I'm thinking about the game from the moment I wake up. I'm trying to prepare myself mentally to eliminate that anxiety and eliminate that anxiousness and eliminate the negative thoughts and try to look on the positive thoughts. Thinking about my plan and thinking about the excitement of going out and competing.

"It's the same for me every single time I take the mound, which is also a thing that I think helped me in that game. Same every game. It's very similar even in Spring Training. That's the way I am. I get excited about that day. I'm excited about competing that game. The feelings inside are the same every day."

From the first inning, Carpenter dealt. He struck out Curtis Granderson on a curveball in the dirt, got Craig Monroe to pop up, and induced a groundball from Placido Polanco. Three up, three down, and 46,513 hyped up. He breezed through another 1-2-3 inning in the second, with a line drive and a pair of grounders. His teammates weren't having much luck with Nate Robertson, but they already knew that if they could get Carpenter even a run or two, they'd be in good shape.

Carpenter wouldn't allow himself to think that way, though. The way he was able to succeed was by not going down that path. Don't think about the last batter, or the next one. Make this pitch, and make it as well as you can.

"I go out and get an out," he recalls. "Get an out. Get an out. I go up the next inning and it's the same thing. I'm not thinking ahead. I'm not getting excited about what's going on. I'm not excited that I got 1-2-3 in the first. I know I've got to go out and make another pitch and get another out. When you can put that all together consistently, you're going to get outs."

Which is not to say that he didn't feel good on the mound.

"From pitch one, I went out and my stuff was there, my competitiveness, my concentration, my adrenaline," he says. "I was able to control everything and I just started pounding my plan in. I knew exactly what I was doing. My pitches were doing what I wanted. I was locating well. And I knew that they didn't have a shot."

Carpenter allowed a single in the third, and thanks to a bunt and a wild pitch, the runner advanced to third base. But he got Granderson to roll over a changeup. Granderson's groundball out to second ended the inning, snuffing out the only semblance of a threat that Detroit could muster all night. Craig Monroe struck out on a curveball to open a 1-2-3 fourth, and in the bottom of the inning, Carpenter got support. Jim Edmonds' two-run double put the Cardinals ahead. Carpenter delivered the shutdown inning in the fifth, allowing a two-out Sean Casey single but striking out two batters.

Carlos Guillen struck out on another curveball for the first out of the fifth, but it's the final at-bat of the inning that stands out. Brandon Inge's strikeout is the only at-bat of the entire game that Carpenter remembers pitch-for-pitch. He pounded Inge down and away for four solid pitches, working a 2-2 count after falling behind 2-0. He finished Inge off with a fastball up and away, as the infielder chased a pitch that was probably a ball.

"I knew if I threw a fastball up out of the strike zone away, because of the sequence that I had pitched him, that I was going to strike him out," Carpenter said. "And I did. I threw it right where I wanted to throw it, just a little bit out of the strike zone on the outside part of the plate, and he swung through it."

If it wasn't Bob Gibson in 1968, it surely was the closest thing St. Louis had seen since the days of "Hoot." Aside from the Inge confrontation, the individual pitches and outs blur together for Carpenter now.

"I don't even remember [what it was like in the dugout]," he says. "I don't talk a whole lot, and when I do, I don't really know what I'm really talking about. I'm just blabbering around. I've had other nights that I was locked in like that, but because of what game it was, it made it that much bigger."

Carpenter rolled on. He needed 10 pitches in the sixth, getting a 4-3 grounder, a 6-3 grounder, and another strikeout of Granderson—this time on a fastball high and outside. With three outs in the air in the seventh, he was six outs away from the World Series win. Two walks and an error in the bottom of the seventh stretched the lead to four runs, and the rest of the game was a coronation for Carpenter.

He wore the crown with grace, striking out Pudge Rodriguez on a cutter before another Casey single. Inge hit into a double play to end the eighth, and Carpenter was done. His last pitch was a sizzling 94-mph sinker that Inge dribbled to third base. He got to hit in the bottom of the eighth but did not pitch the ninth. Not that he couldn't have—Carpenter got 24 outs on a positively Gibson-like 82 pitches, loving every minute of his debut on baseball's biggest stage.

"My work is fun," Carpenter says. "I'm out there smiling and thinking about how fun this is, but making all those pitches and doing all those things and dominating and competing are what it's all about. It was a real enjoyable feeling."

Carpenter was dominating that night, but he was also artful. He threw fastballs at every speed from 92 mph all the way up to 97. He threw two-seam, sinking fastballs and riding four-seam fastballs. He got strikeouts on all four of his pitches. And most of all, he never came over the middle of the plate. Everything was on one corner or the other, and usually both corners within the same at-bat.

"My stuff, my location, the dominant feeling that I had in my mind, was just as good as any other game," he says. "And I continued to get stronger, just like normal. Each inning, each out, each pitch, I continued to get that feeling inside that I knew they had no shot."

It was a dazzling display of throwing, and a masterful exhibition of pitching. Carpenter and catcher Yadier Molina scarcely even needed to discuss their plans or intentions once the game was under way.

"He knows exactly what I'm doing and I know exactly what I'm doing," Carpenter says, "and we're just like, 'Here we go.' Maybe in between at-bats, or during a certain at-bat, I might see something or he might see something as to what pitch we're going to throw. But we know what we're doing. And he knows me well enough and I know him well enough that we know what track and what we want to do with each guy."

Carpenter had pitched like that before. He overwhelmed the Blue Jays in Toronto in 2005, throwing a one-hitter in a memorable homecoming. He shut out the Reds on four hits and no walks just a couple of months earlier in '06. But it's one thing to do it in the regular season, and something else entirely to do it with your team three wins from a world title. It was Carpenter's win, as much as any game in the series, that turned things in St. Louis' favor. The difference is enormous between a 2-1 lead and a 2-1 deficit, something La Russa considered when he slotted Carpenter as the Game 3 starter.

The Redbirds got the next two wins in quick succession. Only a rainout could slow the Cardinals' march to the World Series championship. And when the Cards celebrated at home, it rated as the highlight of Carpenter's career. It's Game 5, not Game 3, that's memorialized in Carpenter's home, and that says pretty much everything.

"That World Series, I still get goosebumps talking about it," he says. "I still look back at it. I have pictures. There's a picture in my house that's right when you walk in the entryway, and it's a picture of me and my wife and my two kids, and I'm holding my son Sam and my wife's holding my daughter Ava.

"The expressions, and the confetti behind us, and Sam's hugging me, and Ava's in my wife's arms not knowing what's going on, that picture tells 1,000 words about the emotion. Not just for the club but for the whole families. Knowing that their significant other or boyfriend or husband or whatever worked so hard to get to that point."

CHAPTER 21

DAVID FREESE

The St. Louis Cardinals have had their fair share of unexpected World Series heroes over the years, including Pepper Martin, John Stuper, and David Eckstein. In 2011, the roster of October surprises grew to include David Freese, a 28-year-old third baseman who quit baseball after high school and wasn't even assured of a regular spot on the Cardinals' roster when the season began.

But Freese's exploits in Game Six brought the Cardinals from near-certain defeat to exhilarating victory, and he delivered again in Game Seven to help St. Louis win its 11th World Series title.

With the Redbirds one strike from a Series defeat in Game Six, Freese rattled a two-run triple off the right field wall to tie the score, then clubbed the deciding home run to straightaway center field leading off the eleventh inning to conclude one of the wildest Fall Classic contests ever played. In Game Seven, he chipped in two walks and a game-tying two-run double.

For his efforts, Freese won the Series MVP trophy and a new black Corvette, the cherry on top of his first full season in the majors. Freese's 2011 was one of valleys and peaks, but in the end glowed in a triumphant blaze of glory.

David Freese was born in Corpus Christi, Texas, on April 28, 1983. He played baseball almost from the time he could walk, and starred at Lafayette High in Wildwood, Missouri, some thirty miles west of St. Louis.

Freese was an outstanding high school player, and as a senior was an All-State selection at shortstop. Years of competitive play had honed his skills, and the University of Missouri offered him a scholarship. Stardom seemed a real possibility.

Then he quit.

"The negativity of the game kind of consumed me," Freese said years later. "I just wanted to do other things, and baseball wasn't one of them. I had been living baseball for fifteen years and I was burnt out. I lost the drive."

Like many young men trained to play ball, Freese felt he'd missed out on just being a kid. He enrolled at Missouri, but refused to go out for baseball. Coaches' entreaties did not bring him back. Even an arranged meeting with Phillies first baseman Ryan Howard—like Freese an alumnus of Lafayette High—did not tempt Freese to pick up a bat.

Instead, Freese took classes, worked odd jobs, and goofed off, drifting, until suddenly getting the itch to return to the field as a sophomore. He did not regret his decision to stop playing—"if I would have kept playing without the desire to continue to play, that would have driven me away from the game," he said—but was happy to don the uniform again. He spent some time at a community college, then transferred to the University of Southern Alabama, where he played alongside future Cardinals hurler P.J. Walters.

Freese was drafted as a third baseman in 2006 by San Diego in the ninth round, and after two seasons in Class A ball, was acquired by the Cardinals in exchange for veteran outfielder Jim Edmonds. Freese, delighted to join his hometown organization, was even happier when promoted from High-A to Triple-A in 2008.

That season at Memphis, Freese batted .306 with 29 homers, proving himself a budding slugger and a strong-armed third sacker.

But the following season he batted just .158 before suffering a seriously sprained left ankle in mid-April. Freese rehabbed the injury and batted .313 in 65 minor-league games, earning a call to St. Louis in September, where he went 7-for-12 with his first big-league homer (on September 29) and five RBI in seventeen games.

David Freese rounds first base after hitting the game-winning home run in Game Six of the 2011 World Series. *APImages*

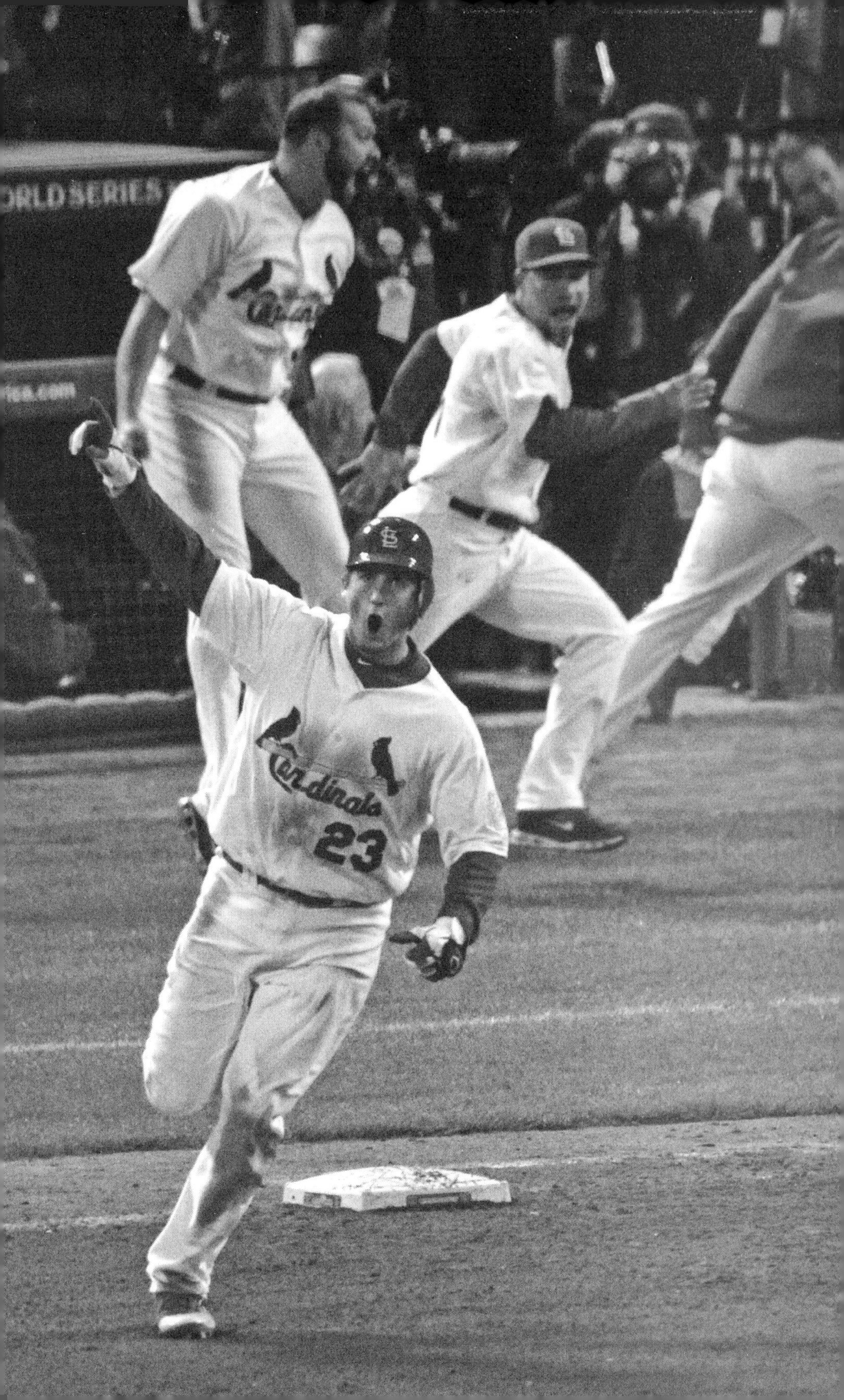
ORLD SERIES
Cardinals
23

That was enough for the Cardinals, who jettisoned their other options and awarded Freese the third base job for 2010.

At 27, he was no spring chicken, but took to the league like a duck to water, batting nearly .300 through May. While Freese hit just four homers in that span, he showed plenty of ability; on April 29 at Atlanta, he homered and drove in six runs.

But on June 5, Freese sprained his right ankle while running the bases against Milwaukee. The injury was serious enough that in late June, the Cardinals placed him on the disabled list. After tearing a tendon in the ankle in a rehab game on August 2, Freese underwent surgery and was shelved for the season.

Entering 2011, the Cardinals did not know if they could count on Freese. So they invited veteran infielders Nick Punto and Ramon Vazquez to camp and added rookie Daniel Descalso to the opening-day roster.

Freese, however, bashed his first home run of the season on April 12 and went deep again two days later. Buoyed by work with hitting coach Mark McGwire and teammate Matt Holliday, who had taken the young third baseman under his wing, Freese hit .375 in April and drove in 14 runs.

Asked about how he was adjusting to the majors, he noted, "I've got some guys behind me, and obviously a few guys ahead of me in the lineup that I just sit and watch and I learn and I soak up everything they do, from Spring Training on.

"I'm with Matt Holliday every day in the offseason. He took me under his wing a couple years ago when things weren't too hot, and he's a big brother to me. I owe him everything."

Just when everything seemed to be coming together for Freese, misfortune struck again. On May 1 in Atlanta, Scott Linebrink of the Braves broke Freese's left hand with an errant pitch, shelving him until June 28.

Descalso played well in Freese's absence, but Tony LaRussa and his staff were happy to welcome Freese back. In July, he homered five times and hit .275. But like most of his teammates, Freese struggled in August, homering just once in a 24-game span and losing 20 points off his batting average over the month.

St. Louis was ten and a half games behind the Atlanta Braves in the wild-card chase on the morning of August 25. But Freese went 3-for-7 with four RBI as his club won three of four at Pittsburgh from August 25–28.

By September 11, the red-hot Cardinals had cut the deficit to four and a half games with a three-game sweep of Atlanta at Busch Stadium. St. Louis kept winning and, improbably, the Braves kept losing.

That month, Freese batted .284 with six doubles and 11 RBI. On the season's last day, with the Cardinals and Braves tied, St. Louis blanked Houston 8-0 at Minute Maid Park while Atlanta fell 4-3 to the visiting Phillies, completing an 8-18 swan dive while St. Louis finished on a 23-9 roll.

Freese, like his teammates, entered the playoffs riding high. He had batted .297 with ten homers and 55 RBI in 96 games, nailing down a regular spot and establishing himself as a bona fide RBI man.

While Freese had proven his mettle, he still struggled with strike-outs and the occasional slump. "Sometimes when you're feeling good at the dish, you get in the habit [of thinking] you can kind of hit everything," he said after the season. "And that's kind of when you get out of whack...you kill your hot streak, this and that, and you've got to kind of zone it back in."

The postseason gave David adequate opportunity to show the baseball world just how well he could zone in.

St. Louis' first challenge was the Philadelphia Phillies, owners of the National League's best regular-season record. With Philly up two games to one, the Cardinals—facing elimination—rallied from a 2-0 first-inning deficit to win Game Four 5-3. With one out and two men on in the fourth, Freese's two-run double to left put St. Louis ahead for good. And his two-run homer in the seventh clinched the win.

The next night, in Philadelphia, the Cardinals captured the series 1-0 behind the masterful pitching of Chris Carpenter.

Freese further burnished his rep in the League Championship Series against the Milwaukee Brewers. He clouted a three-run homer in a 9-6 Game One loss, then homered again and knocked in two runs as St. Louis won the next day.

When the series moved to St. Louis, Freese went 3-for-4 in a Game Three triumph and had two more hits in a Game Four loss. The

Cardinals took control of the series with a 7-1 win in the fifth game, during which Freese singled, walked, and scored twice.

Back in Milwaukee, the Redbirds wrapped up an improbable National League title with a 12-6 thrashing. Freese's three-run first-inning homer started the onslaught, and he added two more hits and scored three runs on the day. Hitting .575 with three homers and three doubles, Freese was an easy choice for series MVP.

The World Series against Texas proved an even bigger and better stage for Freese's game-breaking talents.

In the first game, Freese doubled and walked in a 3-2 Cardinals win at Busch Stadium. The next night, he singled and scored the team's only run in a 2-1 loss.

When the series moved to Texas, Freese and the Cardinals busted loose with a 16-7 slaughter. Freese doubled, singled, walked, drove in two runs, and scored. But Texas won Games Four and Five, holding Freese to just a single in seven trips to the plate.

All of this set the stage for the biggest night of Freese's life—Game Six at Busch Stadium.

It certainly didn't begin auspiciously. He struck out in the first, rolled out softly in the fourth, and in the fifth, with the score tied at 3, dropped an easy pop-up that led to Texas scoring the go-ahead run.

After the game, he commented, "You know, I felt like I was part of a circus out there, bouncing balls off the top of my hat a little bit. But man, I just wanted an opportunity..."

In the last of the sixth, with the score still 4-3, Freese came up with runners on first and second and coaxed a walk out of Colby Lewis, who then gave way to Alexi Ogando. The Rangers righty walked catcher Yadier Molina to force in the tying run.

The immensely talented Rangers, smelling the Series trophy, forged ahead 7-4 in the seventh, scoring three runs off Lance Lynn. Allen Craig's homer in the eighth shaved the deficit to two runs, but Freese grounded out, and it looked like his chance to be a hero was over.

In the last of the ninth, Texas closer Neftali Feliz fanned Ryan Theriot. But Albert Pujols lashed a double to left-center, bringing the crowd of 47,325 to its feet. Feliz, seemingly shaken, then walked Lance Berkman. But Craig took strike three, and the Cardinals were down to their very last hope: Freese.

The Redbirds' third sacker took a ball high, then a fast strike.

"I went up to the dish saying what a great way to have my first career At Bat off Feliz," Freese said. "I just told myself, stay short. He started me off with some off speed, so I was like, now what's coming? I just said, heater, that's the way I hit."

Feliz reared back and blew a fastball right by Freese, and St. Louis was down to its last strike of the season.

"I just looked for something out over [the plate] and swung through a heater," he said, "and then kind of got the same pitch and didn't miss that one."

On Feliz's next pitch Freese swung and connected hard to right field. The ball soared toward the stands. Rangers outfielder Nelson Cruz glided back and reached up, but had misjudged the distance of Freese's drive and couldn't catch it. As the ball bounced off the wall and rebounded toward the infield, Pujols scored with Berkman right behind him. Freese slid headfirst into third, and suddenly the game was tied 7-7.

Busch Stadium was up for grabs. Feliz retired Molina to end the inning, but St. Louis had life.

Texas, not to be denied easily, came out in the tenth and attacked Cardinals righty Jason Motte. With one out, Elvis Andrus singled up the middle, and Josh Hamilton followed with a tremendous home run for a 9-7 Rangers lead.

Did the Cardinals have one more rally in them? Descalso and John Jay both singled to open the last of the tenth, and pitcher Kyle Lohse—pinch-hitting because LaRussa had no position players left—sacrificed them to third.

Reliever Scott Feldman entered the game for the Rangers and got Theriot to roll out, scoring a run but bringing the Rangers within one out of the Championship. But this time the veteran, Berkman, donned the superhero's cape.

Berkman worked Feldman to a 2-2 count. He then turned on a low-and-inside offering and clipped a pop-fly into right-center. With the Rangers outfield playing deep, Berkman's chip shot fell in, and Jay raced home to score the typing run as the crowd exploded again.

Feldman escaped with no further damage. In the top of the eleventh, Jake Westbrook set down the Rangers.

Freese was St. Louis' leadoff man in the eleventh, facing Mark Lowe, the Rangers' eighth pitcher of the contest. In 52 games during 2011, Lowe had fashioned a 3.80 ERA, allowing six homers in 45 innings. Working carefully, Lowe started Freese out with three straight balls.

Reflecting later, Freese recalled that "[I] just worked the count, and I was worried about getting on base, leading off an inning, taking a walk, breaking a bat, single, whatever."

With a 3-0 count, Freese took a fastball for strike one, then fouled back another heater to bring the count full. So far, Lowe had thrown fastballs and sliders, but not his out pitch—the change-of-pace.

"I knew he had a good change-up. So I kind of had that in the back of my head...[then] he threw a change-up—he shook to the change-up—and I got the head [of the bat] out."

While Lowe's pitch was right where his catcher, Mike Napoli, wanted it, Freese swung hard and connected, lofting the ball high and far to straightaway center. Hamilton trotted back to the warning track and sadly watched the ball fall onto the grassy berm beyond the fence, some 420 feet away.

As Freese put his head down and left the batter's box, the crowd began to roar. Rounding first, Freese saw the ball clear the wall and raised his fist. After rounding the bases, he submitted to the ritual beating from his teammates, who tore the jersey from his back.

Interviewed on the field, he laughed, "I'm just glad I had a chance after looking like an idiot on that pop-up."

These Cardinals became the first team ever to score in eighth, ninth, tenth, and eleventh innings of a World Series game.

"We had some good At Bats and we tied it up and just kept battling," noted Freese. "That defines our team, that game, the way we just kept coming back. We've been doing that for a long time...it's incredible to be a part of this."

Following the game, the fan who caught Freese's home run in center field, Dave Huyette, returned the ball to the Cardinals' third baseman. Hours later, Freese was still so keyed up about the contest—and about the upcoming Game Seven—that he was still awake.

"You know, I didn't sleep much because I was so focused on this game...I slept, like, an hour. I was so fired up; I wanted to play that game. You roll on adrenaline this time of year. It's all about knowing that this is the same game as when you're six years old. It's just elevated on a stage, and everyone is watching. But you've just got to keep reminding yourself, it really is the same game and you have a job to do and you try and execute."

Game Seven is what most baseball fans live for. Texas immediately set out to douse the Cardinals' mojo, scoring twice off Carpenter in the first inning.

In the home half, Rangers starter Matt Harrison got the first two Redbirds, but then walked Pujols and Berkman. Enter Freese, who swung at a 3-2 change-up that was a bit higher than it should have been and pulled it to left-center field for a game-tying double.

"You know, when you hit fifth, sixth, seventh, whatever, you hope to hit in the first because good things are usually happening," he noted. "I got up to the plate, had a fairly good idea about what was going to go down, so I took that approach, stuck with it, and got the bat out there and put it in the gap. I think that was a big turning point because it kind of started the game over and got things back to even."

Craig homered in the third to put St. Louis up 3-2. Freese grounded out in the fourth. Carpenter had settled down and was allowing the Rangers nothing

In the sixth, with men on second and third, Freese was intentionally walked to fill the bases, but Feldman walked Molina to force in a run and C.J. Wilson plunked Rafael Furcal to score another for a 5-2 Cardinals advantage.

In what would be his final At Bat of the season, Freese walked in the seventh. Molina followed with an RBI single, bringing the score to 6-2, where it ended. The Cardinals had won their 11th World Championship.

Freese, for his efforts, was immediately named Series MVP. He received a commemorative trophy—and a new black Corvette—on the field from Commissioner Bud Selig following the deciding game.

Asked after the game to reflect, Freese said, "I've tried to soak in this whole postseason as much as I can because you never know if it's your last attempt at a title. You know, it's going to take me a little bit, I think, to realize what we've accomplished.

"And the funny thing is if we [had gone] down tonight and were NL champs, we still did a ton that nobody thought that we could accomplish. And then just to win it is an incredible feeling."

Some doubted that Freese could pull enough pitches and contribute enough power to be a starting big-league third baseman. But Freese set new one-year postseason records with 50 total bases and 21 RBI, and tied the established mark of 25 postseason hits.

Even if Freese never hits another home run in the majors, his name will forever ring in Cardinals lore. But he has more years, more homers, and more big hits in him.

Having worked hard to get where he is, Freese knows his good fortune and great position. "I've had plenty of days of my life where I thought I wouldn't be even close to being a big leaguer. I'm here because of everybody around me. They've put so much trust in me to accomplish not only baseball but just stuff in life, and to do this is…I'm just full of joy, finally.

"I think you've got to kind of take a step back and understand all the work you've put into it, and then you realize how many people are the reason why you're here, starting with my folks. You know, I quit out of high school, and they were the only two people that supported that decision. If I listened to everybody else, I wouldn't be here right now, no chance."

Two days after the Series victory, St. Louis feted its champions with a parade. As he rode along the route, Freese was asked to sum up his feelings. As thousands cheered the motorcade, he simply said, "I'm speechless. This is unbelievable. I'm finally beginning to realize we did something special."